"As a parent of three daughters, I know teenagers fear talking to their parents about difficult subject matters like anxiety and depression. But this no longer has to be the case. My friend David Murray wrote a tool for teenagers to not only help them understand anxiety and depression but also give them guidance on how they can have tough conversations with their parents or other responsible adults."

**Ed Stetzer,** Executive Director, Billy Graham Center for Evangelism, Wheaton College

"David Murray's book and words have been a huge help in my walk with anxiety and depression. As a teenager, a student, and an athlete, the stresses of this world can easily become too much. I'd recommend this book to family, friends, or any teen who is struggling."

**Isaac,** age 17

"Parenting is good for our prayer lives, we find, especially when sons and daughters are navigating the many anxieties that seem to coincide with the teenage years. David Murray has the practical experience and spiritual wisdom to help. Based in biblical truth and at the same time sensitive to the psychological and physiological complexities of human emotions, Murray's companion guides tell real-life stories that empower teens and their parents to understand their feelings, care well for one another, and take concrete steps toward healing together."

**Phil and Lisa Ryken,** President, Wheaton College, and his wife, Lisa

"For years, I have been scouring shelves for solid and practical teen resources that blend Christian faith and mental health. My search is over! In *Why Am I Feeling Like This?*, David Murray offers engaging wisdom that addresses common teenage thought hurdles that perpetuate anxiety and depression, all in a voice that resonates with a teen reader. I am thrilled to add this book to my professional library."

**Emilie DeYoung,** Supervisor for Child and Adolescent Counseling, Family Wellness Center, Zeeland, Michigan

"There are plenty of resources for adults struggling with stress, anxiety, and depression, but few for teens—even though we know that more teens than ever are facing these issues. A resource was desperately needed to address their unique challenges and circumstances, and this book is the best thing I could have imagined. It's the most practical, compassionate, and biblical resource I have ever seen for teenagers struggling with anxiety and depression. I will be quickly recommending this to any struggling teen I know."

**Jaquelle Crowe Ferris,** Founder and COO, The Young Writer; author, *This Changes Everything*

"With anxiety and depression at an all-time high in today's teens, this book could not come at a more crucial time. *Why Am I Feeling Like This?* is an extremely practical, helpful, biblical, and hopeful book that will help open the pathways of communication between teens and their parents. Rather than giving spiritually cliché answers to a complex and multilayered issue, David Murray compassionately walks alongside anxious and hurting teenagers in a disarming way, offering clarity, hope, and wise counsel in how to better understand their unique struggle with anxiety and depression, as well as practical and spiritual tools to take steps toward physical and spiritual healing."

**Sarah Walton,** coauthor, *Hope When It Hurts* and *Together through the Storms*

"All teenagers who experience anxiety or depression long for a silver bullet to magically solve the way they feel. Unfortunately, such a silver bullet does not exist. Fortunately, teens now have a toolbox full of manageable, practical approaches to help them heal in the face of anxiety or depression. In *Why Am I Feeling Like This?*, David Murray demonstrates his understanding of teens' struggles and his grasp of practical, biblical paths toward healing. This book will be an immensely helpful guide to any teen who wants to find healing and is willing to take small but significant action steps to achieve it."

**Christopher Walker,** Associate Pastor for Youth Ministry, Westminster Presbyterian Church, Lancaster, Pennsylvania

"Teens, if you are struggling with anxiety, depression, or a combination of the two, you need to read *Why Am I Feeling Like This?* David Murray will help you—he is insightful, biblical, wise, and practical. Heed his words and counsel, and mostly, heed God's word as you seek to battle anxiety and pursue healing through Christ's help and the hope of his gospel."

**Kristen Wetherell,** author, *Fight Your Fears*; coauthor, *Hope When It Hurts*

"In these days of rising anxiety and depression, parents of teenagers need an accessible, empathetic, and wise guide. David Murray's books team up to provide parents and teens with a way to communicate hope and give grace to one another in these perplexing struggles. Pastors and youth workers will find in Murray a patient and seasoned coach in their efforts to care for anxious and depressed teens and their parents."

**David Sunday,** Lead Pastor, New Covenant Bible Church, St. Charles, Illinois

# WHY AM I FEELING LIKE THIS?

**Other Crossway Books by David Murray**

*Exploring the Bible: A Bible Reading Plan for Kids*

*Exploring the Bible Together: A 52-Week Family Worship Plan*

*Meeting with Jesus: A Daily Bible Reading Plan for Kids*

*Refresh: Embracing a Grace-Paced Life in a World of Endless Demands* with Shona Murray

*Reset: Living a Grace-Paced Life in a Burnout Culture*

*Why Is My Teenager Feeling Like This? A Guide for Helping Teens through Anxiety and Depression*

# WHY AM I FEELING LIKE THIS?

A Teen's Guide to Freedom from
Anxiety and Depression

David Murray

**:: CROSSWAY®**

WHEATON, ILLINOIS

*Why Am I Feeling Like This? A Teen's Guide to Freedom from Anxiety and Depression*

Copyright © 2020 by David Murray

Published by Crossway
      1300 Crescent Street
      Wheaton, Illinois 60187

Published in association with the literary agency of Legacy, LLC, 501 N. Orlando Avenue, Suite #313-348, Winter Park, FL 32789.

Cover Image and Design: Crystal Courtney

First printing 2020

Unless otherwise indicated, Scripture quotations are from the ESV® Bible (The Holy Bible, English Standard Version®), copyright © 2001 by Crossway, a publishing ministry of Good News Publishers. Used by permission. All rights reserved.

Scripture references marked NKJV are from *The New King James Version*. Copyright © 1982, Thomas Nelson, Inc. Used by permission.

Trade paperback ISBN: 978-1-4335-6718-6
ePub ISBN: 978-1-4335-6721-6
PDF ISBN: 978-1-4335-6719-3
Mobipocket ISBN: 978-1-4335-6720-9

**Library of Congress Cataloging-in-Publication Data**

Names: Murray, David, 1966– author.
Title: Why am I feeling like this? : a teen's guide to freedom from anxiety and depression / David Murray.
Description: Wheaton, Illinois : Crossway, 2020. | Includes bibliographical references and index.
Identifiers: LCCN 2019042089 (print) | LCCN 2019042090 (ebook) | ISBN 9781433567186 (trade paperback) | ISBN 9781433567193 (pdf) | ISBN 9781433567209 (mobipocket) | ISBN 9781433567216 (epub)
Subjects: LCSH: Anxiety—Religious aspects—Christianity. | Depression, Mental—Religious aspects—Christianity. | Depression in adolescence—Religious aspects—Christianity. | Teenagers—Mental health.
Classification: LCC BV4908.5 .M87 2020 (print) | LCC BV4908.5 (ebook) | DDC 248.8/3—dc23
LC record available at https://lccn.loc.gov/2019042089
LC ebook record available at https://lccn.loc.gov/2019042090

Crossway is a publishing ministry of Good News Publishers.

LB       30   29   28   27   26   25   24   23   22   21   20
15   14   13   12   11   10   9   8   7   6   5   4   3   2   1

To Joni and Amy,
my beautiful teen daughters

# CONTENTS

# Introduction
# WHY AM I FEELING LIKE THIS?

Freedom! We long for it and love it. At last, free to be and do what we want. That's the teen years, right?

Our first car, our first job, our first date, our first road trip. These are wonderful moments of increasing independence that we experience in our teen years as our parents gradually release us from their supervision. Freedom is so amazing, isn't it? We can't get enough of it, and we can't get it early enough.

But for some of us, our teen years are the opposite of freedom. They are years of increasing bondage. It's not that an outside force like our parents or teachers imprisons us. No, it's an inside force that restricts us. Our own thoughts and feelings hold us captive, and we can't break free from them.

Anxiety and depression lock us up and cast us down. Darkness and panic stalk us and steal our joy and peace. Our teen years feel more like solitary confinement than newfound freedom. "Why am I feeling like this?" you ask. "How do I get out of this?"

This book answers these questions. It will not only explain why you feel like this; it will also equip you with keys to unlock the chains of anxiety and depression. These keys are God-given truths, tools, and tactics that will, with God's blessing and help, release new liberty, peace, and joy into your life.

I've seen this happen again and again in depressed and anxious teens, and therefore I have great hope for you too. I've also used these keys in my own life when I've been sad and anxious, so I know they work from personal experience.

## Anxiety and Depression?

You might be wondering why one book would try to deal with both anxiety and depression. Aren't they different problems? While there are differences, many experts now view them as two sides of the same coin, or two faces of one basic problem.

Yes, someone can be depressed but not anxious, or anxious without being depressed, but about half of all teens who have one also have the other to some degree. As anxiety is more common than depression for teens, and it usually comes before depression, the primary focus of the book will be anxiety. However, many of the keys work for both anxiety and depression, as we will see.

## Personal Stories

We'll meet a number of teens in the coming pages who have experienced different kinds of anxiety and depression. We'll listen to their stories, discover what helped them, and try to learn lessons from what they went through.

In most cases, I've highlighted the main key that helped each teen. However, it's rarely just one key that does the job. Usually a number of keys working together are the best approach. Also, just because the story might be about a guy doesn't mean the lessons from his story aren't for girls. Same goes the other way too. As you read the stories, think about who you most identify with. There may be more than one.

## Normal Stories

One of the reasons I tell you these stories is to show how many teens have experiences similar to yours. About one in three teens experience distressing and even disabling anxiety. In fact, it's now the most common issue for which teens seek counseling. Nearly a third of thirteen- to seventeen-year-olds will experience an anxiety disorder (38 percent of girls and 26 percent of boys).

When it comes to depression, 13 percent of twelve- to seventeen-year-olds experience major depression in any one year, with depression affecting about 20 percent of adolescents by the time they become adults. That's every fifth person in your class! So you're quite normal. There's no need to hide in shame.[1]

## Homework

I wish I could tell you that just reading the chapters will release you from anxiety and depression. It won't. You have to pick up the keys and use them. That's why at the end of each chapter you'll find a Bible verse to memorize, a prayer, and some exercises. You don't need to do all the exercises, but pick the ones you think will be most useful to you.

## Patient

I can't promise you immediate and complete freedom. Anxiety and depression are strong and stubborn forces. It usually takes some time for the keys to work. That means you need patience and perseverance, and you should pray for that. It's a process more than an event. For some of us, the best outcome will be reducing the intensity or duration of anxiety and depression by learning how to manage and respond to it better. And for most of us, if we use the keys God has provided, we can experience significant improvement and have peace and joy more often. If we aim at progress, we can celebrate every small victory.

## Team Approach

You may feel that the adults in your life don't understand your pain. Others want to help but sometimes say or do things that

1. See "Anxiety Disorder Definitions," National Institute of Mental Health, https://www.nimh .nih.gov/health/statistics/any-anxiety-disorder.shtml; and "Major Depression," National Institute of Mental Health, https://www.nimh.nih.gov/health/statistics/major-depression.shtml#part_155031.

make things worse rather than better. That's why I've written a companion book on the same subject for parents, pastors, and teachers: *Why Is My Teenager Feeling Like This? A Guide for Helping Teens through Anxiety and Depression.* Why not ask your mom or dad, or your pastor or a teacher, to read that book and join you on this journey? God has designed us to need others, and you will make much faster and better progress if you have someone walking together with you through this.

I also encourage you to check in with your doctor and a Christian or biblical counselor, or another mental health professional, as this book only covers the basics and the most common kinds of anxiety and depression. You may need the more specialized help a doctor or another specialist can provide or put you in touch with. They will help you build a support team and make a step-by-step plan.

If you are thinking about harming yourself, you must reach out to a trusted adult or call this toll-free number for the National Suicide Prevention Lifeline, available twenty-four hours a day, every day: 1-800-273-TALK (8255).

## TURNING THE KEY

It's helpful to honestly identify your thoughts and feelings and put a label on them. Circle some of the words that describe your anxiety:

| | | | |
|---|---|---|---|
| Stressed | Afraid | Edgy | Panicky |
| Freaking Out | Angsty | Nervous | Shaky |
| Nauseated | Apprehensive | Fidgety | Desperate |
| Worried | | | |

Circle some words that describe your depression:

| | | | |
|---|---|---|---|
| Sad | Lonely | Empty | Hopeless |
| Failure | Gloomy | Suicidal | Painful |
| Exhausted | | | |

**Write out and memorize Psalm 94:19.**

_____

_____

_____

_____

**Prayer**

*God of truth, help me to be truthful as I start this book. Help me to be honest with myself and you about what I'm thinking and feeling. And help me to reach out for help. Amen.*

# 1

# CIRCULAR SARAH

My junior year started off great. I got into the varsity soccer team, and we had a great season. We even made the playoffs. That's when my troubles began. There were lots of extra practices, games, and pressure. I'm one of the younger players on the team, and my teammates criticize me when things go wrong. They don't really want me on the team.

It's taking me longer and longer to get to sleep because I can't stop thinking about what the other girls think about me. Exams are coming up, and I'm so behind. I go round and round the same things in my head. I'm just exhausted with it all. I feel horrible, like I'm going to be sick all the time. I don't know what's happening to me, and I don't know what to do. Am I going crazy?

—*Sarah*

## The Key of Understanding

One of the reasons anxiety and depression are such horrible experiences is that they make us feel out of control. A force bigger than ourselves takes over, and we feel like helpless victims. We don't know what's happening or when it's going to strike next. Life becomes so confusing and terrifying.

Although depression and anxiety feel like a jumbled mess of stuff, there is usually an order to them. And if we can figure that out, we won't panic when we experience them again. We'll also be able to process these horrible feelings better the next time we have them. We'll say, "It's okay. I know what's happening here, and I know how to respond."

Perhaps you can remember the first time you were standing in the ocean and saw a big wave coming. It was terrifying. You didn't know what was going to happen. Now, though, when you see a big wave, you know what's happening and so you don't panic. Instead you brace yourself, take a deep breath, feel the wave as it passes, and then relax. That's where we want to get with our waves of anxiety and depression. So let's try to understand the *worry > anxiety > stress cycle* that Sarah was experiencing.

## WORRY

Worry can be a good thing—in short and small doses. Worry occurs when our minds anticipate a specific problem and spend a limited time thinking about how to avoid it or solve it. For example, when you have an important exam coming up, you worry about passing, which makes you set aside enough time to study.

This is "good" worry. You face a challenge, think about how to meet it, and take the right actions to succeed. It's "good" worry because it comes at the right time, for the right reason, to the right degree, and helps you pass. This kind of worry is nothing to worry about and is a normal part of growing up. You can actually view this kind of stress as your ally and friend. So say to yourself, "This is horrible, but I can handle it with God's help, and it will ultimately make me tougher and better."

Worry is a bad thing when it becomes too big, it lasts too long, or it paralyzes you. It's when thinking about that exam overwhelms and terrifies you so much that you can't study or sleep, or when your mind goes into overdrive. "If I don't get an *A*, then my GPA will drop, and my parents will be mad because I won't get a scholarship, and they can't afford to pay my tuition, and I'll end up with massive debt, and no guy will want to marry me, and I'll be unhappy for the rest of my life."

Out of breath yet? So is your mind—especially because you haven't thought this just once; you've thought it a hundred times today. All because you imagined you got an *A–* instead of an *A* on one exam.

Do you see how, based upon one little possibility, one "what-if," you have rewritten your whole life story in your mind? That's bad worry, and if left unchecked, what usually happens next is anxiety.

## ANXIETY

After worrying *thoughts* come horrible *feelings*. The emotions of fear, dread, and terror begin to grow. We feel on edge, fidgety, jittery, jumpy. We have a sense of impending doom. Worrying thoughts have produced anxious feelings.

But here's a strange thing. Some of us skip the worry step and go straight to anxiety. We are not thinking or worrying about anything specific, and yet we are plagued with a general sense of anxiety. It's come out of nowhere, it's not focused on anything, and it goes on and on. This is often called generalized anxiety.

Sometimes we experience slow-growing, low-grade, back-ground anxiety. Other times it's sudden, in-your-face, and overwhelming. But generalized anxiety is just as painful as worry-caused anxiety. Perhaps it's even more painful, because we often can't identify a specific cause for it.

As we'll see in some of the following chapters, there are causes of this general feeling of anxiety, but they are not as easy to iden-tify as the anxiety caused by specific worries. But whether the causes are specific or general, all this overactivity in our thoughts and feelings, all this worry and anxiety, usually impacts our bodies in the form of stress. That's the next step in the cycle.

## STRESS

If worry takes place in our *thoughts*, and anxiety in our *feel-ings*, stress is what results in our *bodies*. Our worried thoughts and anxious feelings multiply to produce frightening effects in our bodies: heart racing or pounding, breathlessness, headaches, trembling, tension, dizziness, twitching, stomach cramps, nausea, exhaustion, restlessness, insomnia, tightness in the chest or throat, and so on.

This all starts a never-ending loop because we start worrying about these physical symptoms: Am I seriously ill? Am I going to die? Am I going mad? This worry, of course, creates more anxiety and more stress, and so the *worry > anxiety > stress cycle* goes around again and again.

## DEPRESSION

So where does depression come into this? For teens, depression often grows as the *worry > anxiety > stress cycle* grows bigger and faster. Depression is partly the result of the mental, emotional, and physical exhaustion caused by anxiety. It's the dark sense of hopelessness that we'll never get out of this vicious cycle. We give up even trying and sink into deep darkness, which, in turn, actually adds fuel to the *worry > anxiety > stress cycle*.

However, depression can also come first. That's especially the case if we have experienced serious illness, bereavement, trauma, and other sad events. We have a disabling sadness where we're down all the time. We can't sleep, we can't eat (or we can't stop eating or sleeping). We have difficulty concentrating and making decisions, and we feel worthless and hopeless, so much so that we might want to harm ourselves. This often starts off the *worry > anxiety > stress cycle*.

———————————— **Update from Sarah** ————————————

It was a breakthrough for me when I heard about the *worry > anxiety > stress cycle*. It made so much sense of my experience. It was exactly what was happening to me. That cycle started in my thoughts, went to my feelings, then my body.

My counselor told me to try and look at my feelings as an outside observer of them. Instead of getting on the roller coaster of my feelings, I think of myself as watching the roller coaster and describing it to a friend.

Now, when I sense the cycle is beginning, I say to myself, "Get off the roller coaster and watch it instead." That's what I try to visualize in my mind. Sometimes it stops the roller coaster. Other times the roller coaster ride doesn't last as long or doesn't feel so bad. The ups and downs are not so scary.

When I find myself going over and over something someone said to me or about me, I visualize myself putting the words in a box, sealing it with tape, and putting it on a shelf with lots of other boxes. It's another trick my counselor taught me. When I'm tempted to start thinking about it again, I just say to myself, "No, that box is on the shelf, you're not taking it down again."

I've also learned about what my limitations are, and I cut back on the number of activities in my life. I was cramming too much into my days, putting myself under unnecessary pressure for too long.

## TURNING THE KEY

The next time you feel anxious or depressed, use the key of understanding. Try to view your feelings as an outside observer and briefly describe what you experience in your thoughts, feelings, and body. Instead of getting on the roller coaster, try to think of yourself as a spectator watching it from the sidelines and you are calling your friend to describe it. This may not immediately change your feelings, but it changes the way you relate to them. Write down:

- What are my thoughts?
- What are my feelings?
- What is happening in my body?

What was the sequence? What came first, second, and third? Labeling and describing our thoughts and feelings like this reduces their power over us.

**Write out Psalm 56:3 and memorize it.**

_____

_____

_____

_____

**Prayer**
*My Creator, I see how you have made me in a way that my thoughts, feelings, and body are all connected. Help me to observe this calmly and understand this better. Also, teach me to trust you when I am afraid or down. Amen.*

# 2
# TENSE TOM

I'm uptight all the time. I can't relax. I get headaches and back pain, and sometimes feel stiff and sore all over. I think it's partly because I spend most of the day sitting down. I drive to school, I'm sitting at school all day, I drive home, and then spend hours at my desk studying. I'm so tense that I don't sleep well either. I drink lots of coffee to help me study late.

My pastor noticed how unhappy I was and asked me how I was doing. We both agreed that a lot of my unhappiness has to do with my worries about my mom, who's being treated for cancer. He gave me some Bible verses to think on as a help to trusting God with my mom. But he also encouraged me to speak to my doctor.

—Tom

## The Key of Exercise

God has made us in such a way that our emotional and mental health are connected to our physical health. Each affects the other. That's why we need to work on our physical health if we want to improve our emotional and mental health. Our modern lifestyles are not helping us here. We spend 90 percent of our waking time sitting in various seats.

Tom's doctor has been concerned about this sitting lifestyle among his patients for a long time. Sitting too much throughout the day doesn't just weaken people physically. He's seen many younger people like Tom who also suffer mentally and emotionally as a result.

He did some research and found that exercise expels bad mood chemicals from our brains and stimulates happy mood chemicals. It also grows our brains! Tom's doctor developed this simple five-step plan to improve the physical, mental, and emotional health of teens like Tom.

### STEP 1: STAND UP

One of the simplest things we can do to improve our health is get a stand-up desk. You can get an inexpensive one that sits on top of an existing desk. This can be easily raised or dropped every hour or so to give a good mixture of standing and sitting.

### STEP 2: WALK OUTSIDE

Some Scottish doctors are now issuing nature prescriptions for anxiety and depression. That's because walking outdoors for just twenty to thirty minutes a day can do wonders for our overall health. You can do a gentle jog too, but don't make it a performance thing. The main aim is to relax the body, not push it to its limits. Do it at the same time every day so that it becomes a habit.

### STEP 3: WEIGHTS

Get some light to medium weights at a sports store and watch some YouTube videos so you can use them safely. Then, every hour or so, take a break from your studies, do a few minutes of reps, and then get back to the books. This will improve your studies as well as your feelings.

If you're really interested in physical activity, why not join a local gym and get some personal training? Two or three vigorous sessions a week in the gym is a great way to release pent-up tension, emotion, and aggression.

### STEP 4: SPORTS AND HOBBIES

One of the best ways to exercise is to play a sport. Unfortunately, many teen sports today are overorganized and overpressured. The focus on success takes over and all the fun is lost as people become overtrained and overstressed about winning. Pick-up soccer or basketball are excellent ways to exercise and socialize without oppressive pressure. Hobbies can also help relax us, especially ones that are creative or get us outside and moving our bodies.

## STEP 5: EAT HEALTHY

There's no point in doing really good on the exercise front if we then throw junk into our mouths. Diet is just as important as exercise for physical health. Science has shown that what we put in our mouths affects not just our bodies, but also our thinking and feeling.

A balanced diet that has a good mixture of carbs, protein, and fat in the right portion sizes is all that's required. Again, you don't have to aim too high. And just like exercise, try to be as regular and routine as you can in your eating habits.

And that's it: a five-step plan to healthy bodies, healthy minds, and healthy feelings.

## Motivation

I'm grateful to Tom's doctor for sharing this simple plan. In addition to the scientific motivation, I'd like to add some biblical motivation to help you get started.

The Bible persuades us to pursue physical health by the way it connects healthy bodies with healthy emotions (Proverbs 17:22), and by the command to steward and manage our bodies for God's glory (1 Corinthians 6:20). As for our diet, every time we put something in our mouths, we should ask, "Does this glorify or honor God?" (1 Corinthians 10:31).

---
### Update from Tom
---

My mom is still very sick. It makes me sad to see her so weak, and I get worried when I think about the future. However, I am doing much better. When I get home from school, I go for a short walk to wind down and decompress before I start on my books. I got a stand-up desk, and I put it up and down every hour or so. I'm actually studying much better and don't need so much time to finish my homework.

I started working out at home a few times a week, but I didn't keep it up. Then a friend asked me if I would go to the gym with him. We now go three times a week and push one another along. I feel so good afterward. The exercise relaxes me, and I don't feel so angry now. When I feel tense during the day, I do some stretching exercises. I don't need to go to the gym for that.

Doing all the exercise has also made me want to eat and drink better. I've cut out caffeine and sugar and try to eat a lot healthier.

My pastor taught me the *Now-Here-This* exercise: This is a phrase that I say to myself to stop my mind from racing ahead to the future and imagining what might happen to my mom. As I say *Now*, I try to focus on the present, not the past or the future. When I say *Here*, I try to focus on the place I'm in, not anywhere else. *This* tells me to describe what my senses are experiencing right now. What am I seeing, hearing, smelling, and feeling in this moment? I do this quite a few times a day to still my mind and relax my body.

## TURNING THE KEY

1. Choose a set time when you are going to walk (or gently jog) outside each day. Put it in your schedule and keep to it. Focus on your surroundings rather than yourself. Look around you and notice what you are seeing, hearing, and smelling.
2. Use an app like MyFitnessPal to give you regular reports on where you can improve your diet.
3. If your mind tends to race to the future or rake over the past, use the *Now-Here-This* technique to get your mind in the present and relax your body. You might say to yourself, "I see the picture hanging on the wall. I feel my feet resting in my shoes on the floor. I hear the clock ticking. I smell supper cooking," and so on.

Another way to get your focus on the present is to answer these questions out loud: What five things do you see? What four things do you hear? What three things do you feel on your skin? What two things can you smell?

**Write out 1 Corinthians 6:20 and memorize it.**

_____

_____

_____

_____

**Prayer**

*God, you are an amazing Creator. You are interested in my body and have called me to honor and please you with my body. I confess that I have not always done that. Forgive me and enable me to exercise, eat, and drink in ways that glorify you and do me good. And help me to live in the present not the past or the future. Amen.*

# 3
# DOOMED DAVE

Dave is me, your friendly author. Yes, this is my story. I too suffered with anxiety in my teens. Most of my fear was the result of knowing that I was living a life of rebellion against God. Many Sunday nights, I would struggle to fall asleep because I had heard a sermon that reminded me of my terrible spiritual state and where I was going if I died. I wanted to be a Christian . . . but later. I wanted to sin for a few more years. I was taking a terrible risk, and my anxiety and unhappiness reflected that. I knew that I was doomed if I died.

By the following Tuesday or Wednesday, most of my fears had faded, and I was back to sinning again. But I was living under a dark cloud and could never find happiness. Then Sunday would come around, and the fear would start over.

By my late teens, I was living a very worldly life and trying to find happiness in sinful pleasures, which only made me sadder. My life was a mess, and so were my emotions. After many Friday nights with my friends, I would end up back at my apartment and cry myself to sleep with promises of reformation. I was so scared that I would die in my sleep and go to hell. But Saturday morning dawned, and my resolutions soon evaporated.

In my early twenties, the Lord Jesus broke through my rebellion and powerfully saved me from my sins. I experienced peace and joy in an unforgettable way, and I want you to do the same.

—*Dave*

## The Key of Christ

I am going to tell you what Jesus Christ did for me when he saved me, with the hope that you will want to experience this, too, by faith.

### CHRIST GIVES FORGIVENESS INSTEAD OF GUILT

Much of my anxiety was caused by unforgiven sin. I had done wrong, I knew I deserved to be punished by God, and I knew punishment was coming. Consequently, I suffered the stomach-churning fear of guilt and shame, sometimes as I sinned, and always after it.

But by trusting in Christ's death on the cross, where he suffered the punishment I deserved, my sins were fully, freely, and forever forgiven. Christ forgives *all* sin, even when our feelings tell us we have done something unforgivable. Through his word Jesus says, "Your sins are forgiven " (Luke 7:48). That kind of peace is available to you today through faith in Jesus Christ.

### CHRIST GIVES PERFECTION INSTEAD OF FAILURE

How happy would you be if you had a perfect life? That's what Jesus Christ offers you in the gospel. The word for *perfection* in the Bible is "righteousness." *Righteousness* means a right life, a life that matches God's holy standard. That's what Christ lived. But he didn't just live it for himself. He also offers it to us as our own (2 Corinthians 5:21; Romans 5:19).

Having Christ's perfect life as my righteousness gives me perfect peace because now I don't have to try obeying my way to peace. I don't need to try to be perfect anymore. Christ's perfection is my perfection so that I now have peace with God and rejoice in hope (Romans 5:1–2).

Some days I feel good, other days I feel terrible. But Christ's perfect righteousness never changes, which means that my salvation and acceptance with God never changes either. That kind of perfect righteousness and peace is available to you today through faith in Jesus Christ.

## CHRIST GIVES PURPOSE INSTEAD OF AIMLESSNESS

In my teen years, when I was far away from God, I was very ambitious. However, my ambitions kept changing. I was all over the place with no settled sense of purpose or aim in life.

But when I became a Christian, I immediately sensed a clear life-purpose—following and glorifying Christ in everything. This aim was so clarifying. No longer was my life all about self-promotion; it was about Christ-promotion (John 3:30).

And when I asked God for specific direction, "What do you want me to do?," he made that clear too. Now when things don't go according to my plans, I know God has a better plan for me (Romans 8:28). You can have this assuring purpose and stabilizing peace today if you love Jesus.

## CHRIST GIVES CONTENTMENT INSTEAD OF GREED

No matter how much I earned, I always wanted more. I was always striving for more money, a better car, better vacations. No matter how much I possessed, I was always restless. I never had enough.

But Christ changed all that. When I got Christ, I got everything. It doesn't matter if I lose money or experience poverty. I have Christ, the most valuable possession in the world. If you have Christ, you too can enjoy that joyful contentment instead of stressful coveting (Philippians 4:12).

## CHRIST GIVES OBEDIENCE RATHER THAN REBELLION

The Greek word for *sin* in the Bible means "lawlessness." It begins with putting aside God's law and ends in chaos and disharmony. It disturbs inner peace and outer peace. It creates stress and mess. Lawlessness produces lawlessness. That was my life—lawless inside and outside. I knew that, but I couldn't stop it, no matter how hard I tried at times.

But when Jesus saved me, he not only forgave my sins, he gave me his powerful Holy Spirit. The Holy Spirit gives us the power to say no to sin, and yes to what is right. Our lawless chaos is then replaced with peace and order, inside and out.

## My Update

I've been a Christian now for thirty-two years. Although there have been ups and downs, Christ's peace has remained the foundation of my life. I've come close to dying twice with life-threatening illnesses. But even in these moments, Christ's peace was more powerful than my fears. I knew I was going to heaven even if the worst happened.

Perhaps your anxiety also has a spiritual cause. You don't know Christ as your Savior. You know you are doomed if you die. You may not be living such an outwardly sinful life as I was, yet you fear you are not right with God. That spiritual fear and uncertainty may be the root cause of many other anxieties and sorrows. If that is true of you, then until you put this right, you won't get deep, lasting peace or joy.

Jesus sees our spiritual restlessness and calls us to himself: "Come to me, all who labor and are heavy laden, and I will give you rest" (Matthew 11:28). Repent of your sin and believe in Jesus Christ to start tapping into the peace and joy he alone can give.

And remember, Jesus himself has been touched with the feeling of our weaknesses (Hebrews 4:15). He has known overwhelming fear and sorrow (Luke 22:44; Matthew 26:36–42). You can therefore tell him all about your life, knowing that he understands and sympathizes with you.

## TURNING THE KEY

1. Sometimes it helps to put our fears or anxieties into categories.
   - *Physical fears:* Is he, she, or this going to hurt me? Am I seriously ill?
   - *Social fears:* What do they think about me?
   - *Spiritual fears:* Am I a Christian? What if I'm not really saved?
   - *Psychological fears:* These are usually imaginary or exaggerated fears. The fear is based more in our mind than in reality.

   Doomed Dave had spiritual fears. What fears do you have? What categories would you put them into?
2. The most common place to meet and find Jesus is in the Bible. So why not start reading one of the Gospels?

**Write out Matthew 11:28 and memorize it.**

_____

_____

_____

_____

**Prayer**
*Great God and gracious Savior, show me and give me Jesus so that I can experience the peace and joy of forgiveness, perfection, purpose, contentment, and obedience. Amen.*

# 4

# IMAGINATIVE IMOGEN

I don't know why, but my mind is always drawn to sad and painful stories. When I hear of something bad that's happened, like a school shooting, I can't stop thinking about it and imagining myself in that situation.

But even in my own life, I'm always thinking the worst is going to happen to me and to others I love. It's like a nonstop horror movie running on a loop in my mind. Even though the things I imagine never happen, I can't stop seeing the most horrible pictures in my head. It makes me worried and sad all the time.

—*Imogen*

## The Key of Imagination

Maybe you're like Imogen. You have a runaway imagination that is always creating worst-case scenarios, even though they rarely happen. You need to retrain your imagination, as Imogen did. So let's work at replacing disturbing images with God-given images of truth.

I call this image therapy, or imagination therapy. But I didn't invent it; Jesus did, in Matthew 6:25–34. Although Jesus is addressing anxiety in this passage, the same image therapy also works for depression.

### WORRY IMAGES

In Matthew 6:25, Jesus described images of worry in people's minds—what to eat, what to drink, and what to wear. Basically he looked inside people's heads and saw that they were running the same movie on a loop—the worries of everyday life.

In Christ's day, what to eat, drink, and put on were matters of bare survival and therefore causes of everyday anxiety. In our day, food, drink, and clothes are more often matters of social approval, but are no less causes of anxiety. We worry about the same things but for different reasons. Our worries are no longer about existence, but about performance. We're concerned not about survival, but about approval. As we buy clothes, backpacks, cars, and phones, and as we post pictures on Instagram, we obsess over "What will he/she/they think of me?"

But other images, too, play on a loop in our minds. The most common images that cause worry in teens are:

- *Images of impossible expectations.* Perfectionistic standards set by ourselves, others, and social media create constant stress as we try and fail to reach them.
- *Images of an angry God.* A guilty conscience paints a picture of an angry God who is eager to punish us for our sins and who is forever unhappy with us.
- *Images of past trauma.* Painful events such as childhood abuse, a broken home, bullying, the death of a parent or sibling, and other traumas can be trapped in our minds and relived in flashbacks or nightmares.
- *Images of violence.* Blood-soaked video games, movies, and media coverage of the latest violent stories imprint on our minds and terrify our hearts.

So what's the answer? We can't stop imagining. But we can change our imagining. We can use our imaginations to beat our imaginations. We do that by replacing images of worry and sadness with images of peace and joy. So let's go back to Matthew 6:25–34 and get some examples of image therapy from Jesus. He replaces untrue and unhelpful images with truthful and helpful images.

## NATURAL IMAGES

First, Jesus points his disciples to nature, to carefree birds, and how God cares for them despite how little value they have compared to us (Matthew 6:26). Then he points them to flower-covered fields and says that if God takes time to cover the fields with flowers, will he not take time to clothe you (6:28–30)?

Jesus uses these images from nature and everyday life to show us how unnecessary worry is. But these two images from nature are just samples. Jesus is saying that you should get outside, walk around, take it all in, and let images from nature—the sights, sounds, and smells—stay with you and calm you.

## SUPERNATURAL IMAGES

Jesus also paints supernatural images, images of God's character, to minister peace to us. He tells you to picture God as your heavenly Father (Matthew 6:26, 32) and as your King (6:33). As your Father, he is good, kind, and protective. As King, he is in control and he will win. If I can see God as my Father and King, there is therefore no need to worry.

But again, these pictures are merely suggestive of other therapeutic images of God found throughout the Scriptures. In the Psalms, we read of God as a warrior, a shepherd, a shield, a rock, a tower, and a fortress, and so on. In the New Testament, Christ uses many images to describe himself and replace images of worry. He is the Lamb of God, the bread of life, the water of life, the light of the world, the door of the sheep, the bridegroom, and the vine.

In the sacraments, we have visual symbols of the greatest truths in the world. Baptism portrays Christ washing us from our sins. The Lord's Supper visualizes Christ saving us through the pouring out of his blood and the breaking of his body.

And all of this points us to the most spiritually soothing image of all. The cross of Christ removes guilt and shame and replaces it with peace and joy. For the Christian, this is the most calming and joyful image in world history.

## MULTIPLE IMAGES

Do you see how God has multiplied natural and supernatural images of peace to replace our images of worry and pain? Instead of filling our minds with images from the media and social media, images from the past or images of the future, let's fill up our minds with the images God has provided in the world and in his word.

### ——————— Update from Imogen ———————

For the first time in my life I'm getting my imagination under control. I hadn't realized how much of my stress was being caused by the images I was creating in my mind. I haven't been good at reading my Bible, and so I didn't know that it had so many beautiful images to think about. It's also helped to get out in the yard and open my eyes to the beauty all around me. I'm seeing things I never saw before. The internal horror movies still try to run in my head, but now I can stop them much sooner by thinking instead on the images from nature and the Bible. I'm a happier person now, and people have said I seem much calmer.

## TURNING THE KEY

1. What images dominate and trouble your mind? Practice "thought-stopping" by placing a stop sign in front of your worries when they start and then replacing the anxious thought with a happy image like lying on the beach in summer, hiking in the mountains, or whatever makes you really happy.
2. What images from nature or Scripture can you use to replace harmful images? As you read the Bible, look for new images to view and enjoy.
3. Take a walk in nature and pause to paint your mind with evidence of God's care for his creation.
4. If you can't get into nature, visualize a beautiful scene in your mind and put yourself in it. See it, smell it, touch it, taste it, hear it.

**Write out Matthew 6:26 and memorize it.**

_____

_____

_____

_____

**Prayer**

*I thank you, great heavenly artist, for all the pictures of peace and joy that you have painted for me in your word and in your world. Help me use them to replace the images of worry and sorrow that sometimes run in my mind like a movie. Amen.*

# 5

# PANICKY PAUL

I was raised by godly parents in a strong church, and I've been Christian since I was a young child. I can't remember a time when I didn't love the Lord Jesus. But the last few months have been a real struggle. I've been feeling scared and sad all the time, and I don't know why.

A few weeks ago, hours before my alarm went off, I suddenly woke up feeling terrified. My heart was pounding, and I broke out in a cold sweat. I couldn't get back to sleep and felt nervous and jittery all morning. It's happened a few times now.

I tried reading more of my Bible and praying longer, but it doesn't help. If I were truly a Christian, I wouldn't feel like this.

Last week I had one of these panicky attacks in school. That's when I told my mom about it. She said that she had a similar experience when she was younger. I didn't know this, but her side of the family has quite a lot of depression and anxiety. My mom said that a few months of medication had helped her as a teen. She wants me to talk to our family doctor. I really don't want to be on meds. I've always thought that was for crazy people or unbelievers.

—*Paul*

## The Key of Medication

Paul eventually went to see his family doctor and asked her to explain the role of medication in treating anxiety and depression. As she had done many times, she started with the scary bear story.

## A SCARY BEAR

Imagine you are walking in the woods when you see a bear a hundred yards away. Worse, he sees you. Your body goes into fight-or-flight mode. It starts to react to the danger by pumping fear chemicals like adrenaline and cortisol into your system.

These chemicals sharpen our senses, strengthen our muscles, improve our reaction times, and thicken our blood. All this helps us either to stand and fight the bear, or, more wisely, flee from it.

Although horrible feelings of fear and panic go along with the fight-or-flight response, it's a God-given survival system. It's meant to turn on for just a few minutes, enough for us to either fight the bear and win, or run and escape (or bleed more slowly if we're injured). Then, in about twenty minutes, that system should turn off, and everything in our body goes back to normal.

## AN INVISIBLE BEAR

The problem is that some people's fight-or-flight system turns on when there's no bear there. For other people, perhaps victims of abuse or some other trauma, their fight-or-flight system turns on for a good reason, but stays stuck on and won't turn off. Or perhaps it's activated frequently without any reason at all. There's little or nothing people can do about this. Our bodies are broken, and no amount of faith can fix them. It's a physical problem that needs a physical solution.

Medication can play a role in controlling and rebalancing these chemicals. Sometimes medicine is what's needed to heal our bodies in order to then heal our emotions. This is especially so if our family has a history of anxiety or depression. That's often an indicator that it may be a physical problem passed down through genes.

This should also help us to understand Imogen's story a bit better. She was turning on her fight-or-flight system all the time by allowing her overactive imagination to picture endless scary scenarios.

We need to keep three other important points in mind when we think about medication: God's gift, God's package, and God's blessing.

### GOD'S GIFT

While some anxiety and depression have a spiritual component, some also have a physical component, as described above. Just as God graciously provides the gift of faith to heal our spiritual problems, God has also graciously provided the gift of medications to heal physical problems. Just as we wouldn't go to our doctor with a spiritual problem, we wouldn't go to our pastor for a physical problem. We thank God that he has helped scientists and doctors to discover these remedies. Lots of people in the past had these problems, but there were no meds to help.

### GOD'S PACKAGE

I'm not saying that medication is usually the first key we try or that meds alone will solve our problems of anxiety and depression. Usually medicine works best when used together with the other keys in this book. They are best as part of a package. You can perhaps view them as scaffolding that supports you while you rebuild using the other keys, especially if your depression or anxiety has been intense or long.

### GOD'S BLESSING

Pray about the medication. Ask for God's guidance on whether you should go to the doctor, what to tell him or her, and for the doctor to make the right decisions. Then ask for God's blessing on the meds and on all the other means of healing he has provided.

One last thing: I recommend that if you do take meds, don't tell too many people about it. A lot of people, especially teens, don't understand issues like depression and anxiety. People can say hurtful things about medications for anxiety or depression. There's no point in opening the door for even more stress into your life.

────────────── **Update from Paul** ──────────────

I definitely did not want to be on meds. It did help when my mom told me about her own family's history. I didn't feel so weird after that. But what really helped me was the scary bear story and the understanding this gave me of my fight-or-flight system. I then realized that it wasn't a spiritual problem for me, but a physical problem.

My doctor didn't just give me a pill, though. She talked me through the importance of exercise, good diet, relaxation techniques, going to bed the same time every night, and spending time with friends.

The first medication she prescribed didn't make much difference. After a few weeks I went back to her, and she switched my meds. Within two to three weeks I was feeling quite a bit better.

The fight-or-flight moments gradually reduced in number and intensity, and I started feeling calmer and happier. I'm even enjoying reading my Bible and praying again. After a month, I asked the doctor if I could come off the meds. She said it was too soon but we'd talk again about this in a few months. She's hopeful that will be enough time for the medicine to reset my body's system.

## TURNING THE KEY

Here's a simple summary about the role of medication in treating depression and anxiety.

1. *Don't rush to meds.* Unless your depression or anxiety is especially severe, medication shouldn't be the first key you try.
2. *Don't rule out meds.* Sometimes pride or misunderstanding can make us rule out meds for anxiety or depression. Keep an open and humble mind.
3. *Don't wait too long.* The deeper we sink into the pit, the longer it can take to get out again.
4. *Don't rely on medication alone.* Meds rarely work on their own. What they can do is help you to use the other keys in this book.
5. *Don't expect rapid results.* Some meds take two or three weeks to kick in. Sometimes the first med doesn't work, but a second or third might.
6. *Accept some side effects.* Some meds might produce unpleasant side effects. If this gets too bad, you need to tell your doctor. However, it can be worth accepting a few side effects for a few months if it will remove depression and anxiety in the long run.

**Write out Jeremiah 17:14 and memorize it.**

_____

_____

_____

_____

**Prayer**

*Thank you, Lord, for providing medication to heal my body and its damaged feelings. Help my doctor to know if I need them. If I do, bless them so that they work and enable me to use the other keys better. Amen.*

# 6

# FAITHLESS FLAVIA

I wasn't raised in a Christian family and therefore knew almost nothing about the Bible. Six months ago, in my freshman year at college, a friend asked me to go to church with her. I liked her a lot and said yes. The pastor was easy to understand, and I started going most Sundays. After a few months of this, I understood the gospel, and by God's grace, I put my faith in Christ for the salvation of my soul.

The problem is, I can't seem to trust him with the rest of my life. I trust him to save me, but I can't trust him to care for me. I believe he is my Savior, but I struggle to believe he is my protector and provider. I also get very upset when I see suffering in the world. Can God really be in control when so many people are dying in wars, shootings, earthquakes, and so on? It makes me so anxious.

Last week my pastor preached on the text "I believe; help my unbelief!" (Mark 9:24). That summed me up so well that I went to my pastor afterward for help with my unbelief. If only I could have more faith in God, I wouldn't be so afraid.
—*Flavia*

## The Key of Scripture

Flavia's pastor had counseled many young Christians like her. He knew that the best thing he could do for her was to help her get to know the Bible better. The better she knew her Bible, the better she would know God, and the less she would fear for herself or the world.

He pointed out that the most popular Bible verses in 2018 were about overcoming fear. The YouVersion Bible app reported that the most shared, bookmarked, and highlighted verse in the world was Isaiah 41:10: "Fear not, for I am with you; / be not dismayed, for I am your God; / I will strengthen you, I will help you; / I will uphold you with my righteous right hand."

Two other verses that topped the list in countries like Mexico and Argentina also focused on fear and discouragement:

Have I not commanded you? Be strong and courageous. Do not be frightened, and do not be dismayed, for the LORD your God is with you wherever you go. (Joshua 1:9)

Casting all your anxieties on him, because he cares for you. (1 Peter 5:7)

These statistics tell us that the world is full of anxious people, and lots of them look for help in the Bible.[1]

## THE CHARACTER OF GOD

Flavia's pastor gave her this list of verses that focuses on the character of God, and showed her how these truths can change her feelings. He asked her to read them, think about them, and believe them.

- When you feel out of control, remember God is in control of everything (Job 42:2).
- When you feel weak, remember God is all-powerful (Psalm 147:4–5).
- When you feel helpless, remember God is our helper (Hebrews 13:6).
- When you feel vulnerable, remember God is our protection (2 Thessalonians 3:3).

1. Griffin Paul Jackson, "The Top Bible Verses of 2018 Don't Come from Jesus or Paul," *Christianity Today*, December 10, 2018, https://www.christianitytoday.com/news/2018/december/most-popular-bible-verse-2018-youversion-app-bible-gateway.html/.

- When you feel uncared for, remember God cares for us, and therefore we can cast all our cares upon him (1 Peter 5:6–8).
- When you don't know what's going on, remember God knows everything (Psalm 139:1–4).

Flavia focused on a truth a day over the next week, and was amazed at how, wherever she was lacking, God's character had something to fit her and fill her.

## THE PROMISES OF GOD

The next Sunday, Flavia shared with her pastor how God's word had strengthened her faith. He was pleased with her progress and told her that instead of listening to her anxieties, she was to talk to them with truth. That's because anxieties grow when they are allowed to talk, but shrink when they have to listen. Same goes for depression. The pastor gave her another sheet, titled "God's Promises."

- When feeling lonely, remember God's promise to never leave you or forsake you (Hebrews 13:5).
- When inner turmoil rages, remember God has promised his peace to guard your heart and mind (Philippians 4:6–7).
- When worried about money, remember God's promise to supply all your needs (Philippians. 4:19).
- When stressed about problems in your life or your world, remember God's promise to work all things together for the good of his people (Romans 8:28).
- When drowning in anxiety or depression, remember God's promise that he will not let the waters overflow you (Isaiah 43:2).
- When pessimistic, remember God is optimistic about the future (Rev. 21:3–4).

Again she read one verse a day and even tried to memorize some of them. The pastor was delighted, and encouraged her to look out for more of God's promises and more truths about God's character. But he also gave her a Bible reading plan to help her build the holy habit of daily Bible reading.

──────────── **Update from Flavia** ────────────

I can't believe how much more I believe now! Reading these verses really strengthened my faith. But what made the biggest difference was starting to read a few verses from my Bible every day. I learned more about the character of God and the promises of God. The more I knew, the more I believed, and the more peace I enjoyed.

I especially love the psalms, which describe how the most fear-filled believers moved from anxiety to confidence (Psalms 27; 55; 56) and from depression to joy (Psalms 42; 73; 77). Even the one psalm where depression does not appear to be fixed (Psalm 88) shows us that we can take unfixed depression to God and tell him about it.

In the New Testament I've noticed that although the disciples were often afraid, Jesus was patient with them, forgave them, and transformed them into fearless followers and joyful preachers of the gospel.

Although I still pray "I believe, help my unbelief," belief is getting stronger and unbelief is getting weaker. I'm trusting Christ more now, not just for salvation but for everything. I feel calmer and more hopeful.

## TURNING THE KEY

Here's the advice that Flavia received from her pastor about daily Bible reading.

- *Start reading:* Yes, you've messed up many times, but you've got to start again. So start today.
- *Prioritize reading:* Read the Bible before you pick up your smartphone. Turn off your phone, computer, and email while reading God's word.
- *Routine reading:* Do it the same time, same place, every day.
- *Short reading:* Read for five minutes. Then, in a week or so, increase your time by another minute or so. Aim to get to ten minutes a day.
- *Consecutive reading:* Read one book through. Maybe start with a Gospel, picking up each day where you left off previously.
- *Varied reading:* Once you finish a New Testament book, start an Old Testament book, then back to the New Testament, and so on.
- *Prayerful reading:* Ask God for help and understanding.
- *Concentrated reading:* Do this all with intensity and drive. This is not a time for half-heartedness.
- *Accountable reading:* Ask a friend to keep you accountable, to regularly ask you how it's going.

**Write out Psalm 119:165 and memorize it.**

_____

_____

_____

_____

**Prayer**

*Thank you, Lord, for the Bible and especially for what it tells me about your character, your promises, and your people. Give me faith to trust your word, especially when I feel afraid or down. Help me to read the Bible every day so that I can grow in peace and joy. Amen.*

# 7

# CONTROLLING COLIN

I spend about an hour every night before I go to bed checking that all the doors are locked and the switches are off. Andy, my counselor, believes this obsessional behavior is related to my upbringing. My dad left my mom, my two sisters, and me when I was only three years old. Andy thinks I'm trying to create a safe environment to make up for the loss of security and stability in my life. I've tried to stop doing this stuff, but I get really agitated and angry then.

I don't do well with any changes in my life. I like things to stay the same. So when I started high school last year, I had a difficult time. Everything's so different. People tell me to stop worrying, to stop being so OCD. I've tried hard. It doesn't work. I feel like I'm out of control.

One thing that has helped me is a sermon my pastor preached on Philippians 4:6–7 and the importance of prayer. I've listened to it a few times now online. Here are my notes.

—Colin

## The Key of Prayer

If you were in jail waiting to be executed, you'd be pretty anxious, wouldn't you? Yet when the apostle Paul was in that exact situation, he wrote this:

> Do not be anxious about anything, but in everything by prayer
> and supplication with thanksgiving let your requests be made

known to God. And the peace of God, which surpasses all understanding, will guard your hearts and minds in Christ Jesus. (Philippians 4:6–7)

Amazing, isn't it? Wouldn't we all love to be like Paul when we're in our own emotional prison?

### REPLACEMENT THERAPY

I'm sure we've all had people tell us, "Don't be anxious. Stop worrying." Or, "Don't be sad. Cheer up!" Easier said than done, isn't it?

Notice that Paul doesn't only tell us to stop worrying. He tells us something to do instead of worrying. Yes, he tells us to *stop* something, but he also tells us to *start* something. Unless we start something else, we create a vacuum, and the old worries will just get sucked back into our minds again. So we empty our minds of worry by filling our thoughts with a replacement. And what is that replacement? Prayer.

### OUTSIDE THERAPY

Worry is an internal conversation we have with ourselves. Prayer is a conversation with God. It takes our worry to God and talks to him about it. It adds God to the conversation.

Prayer, therefore, turns us inside out. It takes what's inside us and puts it outside of us. Even just that act can be relieving. That's why many counselors recommend that we write our worries or sorrows on a sheet of paper. It gets what's inside us outside of us. And usually the things that we are worrying about don't look or feel so bad when we see them written out.

But prayer is far more than getting what's inside us outside of us. It's getting what's inside us into heaven! So by all means write out your worries, but then pray them upward.

### LISTENING THERAPY

Perhaps you've tried to talk to someone about your anxiety, but the person has been too busy to stop and really listen to you.

God is not like that. If you want to get God's attention, all you need to do is pray. Prayer stops the God of the universe. It get his full attention. He listens better than any human being ever can. Remind yourself of this when you pray: "God has just stopped to listen to my prayers. I am speaking into the ear and heart of God." We can take *everything* to God in prayer—every worry and sadness.

### THANKFUL THERAPY

Apart from bringing our stress and sadness to God, the most important thing to bring is our thanks. That's why the apostle Paul says that we are to pray "with thanksgiving." Sometimes our anxieties and sorrows are so overwhelming that they're all we see. But Paul encourages us to cultivate a grateful spirit, to look for the good things in our lives that we often miss. Thanksgiving is peace-giving and joy-giving.

### SPECIFIC THERAPY

Philippians 4:6 says, "Let your requests be made known to God." Sometimes our prayers consist of vague generalities. But we can tell God our specific worries and sorrows and give him our detailed requests. What might that look like? "Lord, I'm worried about my history exam. Please give me calm and peace." "Lord, I've lost my joy, and I'm afraid I'll never be happy again. Help me to find joy in you even when there's little in my life to cheer me."

### PEACEFUL THERAPY

How peaceful do you think God is? That's the peace he promises you! God gives his own peace to those who come to him with prayers for peace. Internal peace is a little piece of heaven on earth. It's a little piece of God in our hearts. He doesn't just send peace; he comes himself and is our peace. That's why Paul calls it a peace "that surpasses all understanding."

## PROTECTIVE THERAPY

Some therapies deal only with the past. They try to give people peace about past events and trauma. But Philippians 4:6–7 deals with the future too. God gives a peace that "will guard [future tense] your hearts and your minds in Christ Jesus." Paul pictures God's peace like castle walls that will defend and even rebuild our hearts and minds.

And notice that this is all done "in Christ Jesus." One of the ways God answers our prayers is by making Jesus more real and precious to us. If anxiety and depression take Christ out of the picture, prayer puts him back in.

## Update from Colin

Before I heard my pastor's sermon on Philippians 4, prayer was not part of my life. I was not trusting God or his promises. I was trusting myself and my rituals. I thought I could control my life and my circumstances, but high school showed me that was impossible.

I know people were well-meaning when they told me to stop worrying, but they never gave me anything to do instead. The breakthrough for me came when I realized I needed to do more than just stop something bad. I needed to start something good. That something good was prayer.

Prayer is not like a magic wand that works all the time, but I have experienced more peace since I started replacing controlling with praying. Usually my prayers are simple: "Help me to trust you, Lord!" But a prayer like that is enough to bring God into the picture and change my thoughts and feelings.

I've also learned from my counselor to separate problems into two categories: some problems I can do something about, and others I simply need to accept. I ask myself, "What am I going to do about the ones I can change, and how am I going to manage the ones I can't?"

## TURNING THE KEY

1. Set aside five minutes to pray when you read the Bible in the morning.
2. Follow the ACTS pattern:

   - *Adoration:* Spend a minute or so worshiping God for what he means to you. Remind yourself that he is in control of everything.
   - *Confession:* Spend time confessing your own sins. Admit to yourself and to God, "I am not in control."
   - *Thanksgiving:* Express gratitude to God for his blessings in your life and for his overall control of everything.
   - *Supplication:* Ask for what you are in special need of, then ask for the needs of others.

3. Thanksgiving is especially healing for anxiety and depression. Start a gratitude journal, and every day write down three to five items that you are thankful for.

**Write out Philippians 4:6–7 and memorize it.**

_____

_____

_____

_____

**Prayer**

*Heavenly controller, help me to trust your control of my life. When I'm stressed or sad, remind me to pray. Help me to be specific and thankful in my prayers. May your peace and joy be my peace and joy so that my mind and heart are well-guarded. Thank you for listening to me whenever I pray. Amen.*

# 8

# DEPRESSED DAN

I was a fairly happy kid until middle school. I was always a bit shy and cautious, and sometimes I worried about silly things. In middle school though, worry and fear took over my life. Every time I got sick, I imagined I had cancer. I didn't play sports because I was afraid of messing up or getting an injury.

My dad drinks a lot. It started when my grandma, my mom's mom, came to stay with us a couple of years ago. She has dementia, and it's really stressful for us all. But we can't afford a nursing home. Dad works late a lot now and goes to the bar on the way home. Sometimes he gets really mad. I try to stay out of his way.

I hate going to school because I get bullied a lot. When I'm home, I spend hours in my bedroom. When I'm not playing videogames, I just lie on my bed, hoodie over my head, thinking how life sucks. I don't know why God is doing this to me.

—Dan

## The Key of Elephant Training

Think of your emotions as an elephant. Like an elephant, our feelings can be very strong and damaging if we let them loose in our lives. That's why we need a rider on the elephant to take the reins of our feelings and keep them under control. Psalm 77 helps us understand how our thoughts and feelings are connected, and it helps us do some elephant training.

In the first nine verses, we see that Asaph's emotions were controlling him, causing him terrible trouble. The elephant of his feelings was on the rampage. But by the end of the psalm, we see him at peace. So what happened? Let's follow the psalm to learn from Asaph. Notice, first of all, the sequence of *Trouble* > *Feelings* > *Thoughts* in the first nine verses.

## TROUBLE > FEELINGS > THOUGHTS

*Time of Trouble:* Asaph is facing a time of trouble in his life (Psalm 77:2).

*Forceful Feelings:* The result of the trouble is that Asaph's feelings are all over the place. In verses 1–9, he describes feelings of helplessness, depression, distress, and anxiety. He feels inconsolable, unloved, and forgotten. Although it is good and healthy to verbally express our emotions, these out-of-control feelings are now controlling him and his thinking.

*Terrible Thoughts:* With such feelings in control, it's no surprise that his thoughts are distorted, especially his thoughts about God. God is bad (Psalm 77:3); the past was great but the future is bleak (vv. 5–7); God has abandoned me (v. 7); God's character has changed (vv. 6–7); God has broken his promises (v. 8); and God has no mercy left (v. 9). Do you see how Asaph's emotions are poisoning his thoughts about himself and God? His feelings are determining the truth. The elephant is winning!

*Big Pause:* But at the end of verse 9, Asaph pauses and takes a deep breath. *Selah* at the end of the verse means "stop and be silent." As he does this, his frantic feelings begin to subside, and his thoughts become clearer. He looks back on the previous nine verses as mistaken thinking that was based on his out-of-control emotions.

## TROUBLE > THOUGHTS > FEELINGS

*Remaining Trouble:* As far as we know, Asaph is still facing trouble. But his response to the trouble has changed in verses

10–20. The key is that biblical reasoning is now on the elephant's saddle and taking the reins of his feelings. Instead of *Trouble > Feelings > Thoughts*, the sequence now is *Trouble > Thoughts > Feelings*.

*Biblical Thoughts:* Feeling verbs are prominent in verses 1–9, but thinking verbs are prominent in verses 10–13. "I will remember, I will ponder, I will meditate," and so on. Reason is asserting itself and emotions are being dethroned. Asaph decides he's going to think thoughts about God rather than focus on his feelings. As he begins to meditate on God's character, God's works, and God's word, "I, me, and myself" are receding, and God is in the foreground.

*Changed Feelings:* Although Asaph's trouble has not changed, his thinking has changed, and, therefore, his feelings change. He actually doesn't mention his feelings explicitly in verses 10–20, which indicates they are not so prominent in his life. But they are implied by the tone and content of the remainder of the psalm. We see confidence instead of doubt, optimism instead of pessimism, security instead of fear, comfort instead of distress, clarity instead of confusion, peace instead of anxiety, and joy instead of depression.

Biblically informed and believing reason is now in control, and the psalmist is at rest. He models how to move from emotional thinking to biblical reasoning, from feelings-based thinking to truth-based reasoning. He has used God's word to train and tame the elephant of his emotions.

─────────────── **Update from Dan** ───────────────

I would say I'm about 50 percent better than I was a couple of months ago. I hadn't realized my thinking patterns were affecting my emotions so much. I totally identified with Asaph. The first nine verses of Psalm 77 were my story.

My feelings were controlling my thoughts. When I get into such a hole again, I pause, take a few deep breaths, and say, "Don't let the elephant loose in your life!" It's amazing to know that, with God's help, I can actually now control my feelings.

My counselor encouraged me to think of my feelings as a snow globe. If you leave a snow globe on the table, in a few minutes all the snow that you've shaken up sinks to the bottom, and you can see clearly again. When my feelings get the better of me, I think of the snow globe and wait a few minutes; they often pass, and then I can see clearly again.

There are still tough things going on in my life. I still get bullied. My dad is still drinking. But, like Asaph, I find that I can have peace and even some happiness inside despite what's going on outside.

## TURNING THE KEY

Let's do some elephant training using Psalm 77 to change the sequence from *Trouble > Feelings > Thoughts* to *Trouble > Thoughts > Feelings*.

1. Follow Asaph in expressing your pain and sorrow to God. Don't bottle it up but bring it to him and pour out your heart before him. You may want to write your own psalm that expresses your sadness and your joy.
2. Pause. After letting your emotions out, it's time to get them under control. Breathe deeply and slowly, be quiet, and let your feelings subside a little.
3. Notice how your feelings are affecting your thinking and leading you to faulty conclusions, to bad thoughts. Say to yourself, "Don't let the elephant loose in my life!"
4. Challenge your faulty thoughts with biblical truth. Start thinking about God, his character, his word, his world, and his works, especially his works of redemption in the Old and New Testaments.
5. Notice that as you think about God and his truth, healthy and positive emotions strengthen and replace the painful negative ones, even if the facts of life are still difficult. Your feelings are changing for the better as truth and reason take the reins of the elephant.

**Write out Psalm 77:11–12 and memorize it.**

_____

_____

_____

_____

**Prayer**

*Yes, Lord, I admit it. Sometimes I let my emotions control my thoughts and my life. Teach me how to use Psalm 77 to express my emotions but also to get my emotions under the control of biblical reasoning. Show me how to change my emotions for the better by changing what I think about. Through this, give me a peaceful inside even when storms are all around me. Amen.*

# 9

# NEGATIVE NICOLE

I'm a failure. Nothing ever goes right in my life. Just yesterday, I was snowboarding and learning lots of new tricks. It was going so well. But then I had a wipeout on one of the jumps. A couple of my friends thought this was really funny. I hate them and wish I'd never gone.

Then I came home and got totally stressed out when I thought of all the time I'd wasted on the slopes, and all the things I should've been doing for school. This happens to me every time I go out with friends. I enjoy it at the time, but then hate myself afterward because I know I ought to be studying much harder to keep my GPA up.

—*Nicole*

## The Key of Rethinking

In the last chapter we saw what happens when our emotions control our thoughts. Sometimes, though, our thoughts are the main problem. Our false thoughts become false thinking patterns that drag us down emotionally. That's what was happening with Nicole.

Most of this was not Nicole's fault. She had loving parents, but they had very high standards and were often critical if she fell short in anything. As Nicole grew up, she internalized these standards and criticisms. Her parents' voices became her inner voice. Without realizing it, she gradually adopted their standards and criticisms as her own. The result was a number of false thinking patterns that caused many of Nicole's painful emotions.

I'm going to summarize the most common false thinking patterns (sometimes called "distorted thinking") that I find in teens. See if you can identify the ones that were harming Nicole and the ones that may be harming you too.

## IDENTIFYING FALSE THINKING PATTERNS

*False extremes.* You evaluate people and events in extreme, black-and-white categories. It's sometimes called all-or-nothing thinking. You make a mistake in one part of life, but then conclude you are a failure in every part of your life. You invite some friends over, but one doesn't come, so you say to yourself, "The whole thing was a disaster."

*False generalization.* You have one bad experience, but then presume that the same thing will happen again and again. Your first attempt at public speaking goes badly, so you decide that this will happen every time you try it. "This always happens to me."

*False filter.* You pick out the negative in every situation and think about only that, to the exclusion of everything else. You get 95 percent on an exam, but all you can think about is the 5 percent you didn't get. You filter out anything positive; everything is negative.

*False transformation.* You transform neutral or positive experiences into negative ones. If someone is nice to you, you say to yourself, "She's just feeling sorry for me." If someone wants to hang out with you, you think, "He's just doing that because someone told him to."

*False mind reading.* You think you can tell what others are thinking about you. You imagine that you can read their minds, and you decide that they hate you or view you as stupid. A person doesn't like your Instagram post, so you decide that the person now hates you, despite no evidence to support this. It may be he just never saw your post.

*False fortune-telling.* You are sure things will turn out badly. You expect catastrophe, and the expectation itself produces stress. You make predictions such as "I will fail that exam and it will be a catastrophe." Or you ask lots of what-if questions about the future: "What if I get anxious? What if I panic? What if . . ."

*False shoulds.* Your life is dominated by a multiplying of *shoulds* or *oughts.* "I should do this. . . . I ought to do that. . . . I should be this. . . . I ought to be. . . ." But in most cases these *shoulds* and *oughts* are self-imposed and impossible to fulfill.

*False responsibility.* You assume responsibility and blame yourself for a negative outcome, even when there is no basis for this. For example, when parents divorce, kids often blame themselves and feel responsible for trying to get them back together.

Identifying our false thinking patterns is a huge step forward. Often just being able to see what we are thinking and how illogical and false it is can stop the pattern. But, if it doesn't, we move on to challenging and changing our thoughts. In Dan's case, we used truth from God's word to help him change his emotions and thoughts. But we can also use truth from God's world to change our thoughts and emotions. I'll show you how to do that below.

## CHANGING OUR FALSE THINKING PATTERNS

Think of a court. Put your false thinking pattern on trial. Then bring evidence and witnesses into the court to challenge the false thinking. Ask yourself, "What evidence is there to support this, and what evidence can I bring to challenge it?" Most of the time we can find evidence and witnesses to show how untrue our thinking pattern is. We find it guilty of lying, condemn it to execution, and then replace it with what is true and accurate. As we do, our feelings improve. Let's listen to the conversation Nicole had with her counselor when they put Nicole's thinking patterns on trial.

Counselor: What happened that made you feel so down?

Nicole: I had a fall snowboarding, and all my friends laughed at me.

Counselor: What did you think about that?

Nicole: I'm a terrible snowboarder, and I hate my friends.

Counselor: Let's take the first thought. What makes you think you're a terrible snowboarder? How many falls did you have that day?

Nicole: Only one.

Counselor: And how many jumps and tricks went well?

Nicole: I learned a lot of new tricks and managed some of the hardest jumps.

Counselor: Well, it sounds to me like you actually had a really successful day. Why don't you think more about your successes rather than the one fail? That will give you a much more accurate picture of yourself, and you will feel better too.

Nicole: I see what you mean. I'll try. But I still hate my friends.

Counselor: Okay, let's look at that thought and see if we can find evidence to change the way you're thinking about them. First of all, how many of them laughed at you?

Nicole: There were seven of us, and two of them laughed at me.

Counselor: Only two? So most of them didn't, right?

Nicole: Right.

Counselor: And have the two friends who laughed done anything else to make you mad at them?

Nicole: No, not really. They've always been nice to me. Okay, maybe it wasn't such a bad day after all. But I still felt terrible when I got home thinking of all the schoolwork I should've been doing.

Counselor: Now, Nicole, let me ask you, what truth, what witnesses, can you use to challenge and change your thoughts about the schoolwork you didn't do?

Nicole: Okay, let me try this. I've been working really hard all week. I know if I work too hard too long, I get tired and can't study. So one day off to go snowboarding is good for me and I deserve it after working so hard. Instead of thinking, "I should've been studying," I can think, "I should go snowboarding."

Counselor: Excellent, Nicole. You're going to be a very good lawyer one day!

## —————— **Update from Nicole** ——————

I always feel better after meeting my counselor. She helps me see and change my false thinking patterns, which get me so down. I'm getting better at this court thing myself now.

It's not easy. In fact, it's hard work to change my patterns of thinking. It's much easier just to think like I've always thought. Negative, negative, negative. But this makes me feel so bad, and I don't want to go on like this.

So I work at this every day. In the evening, I take five or ten minutes with my notebook, and try to identify any false thoughts I've had that day. I write them down, and then write down reasons why I should not believe my false thoughts. I usually feel much better after this. And gradually I do feel I'm getting more positive about life.

I've learned to be on the lookout for words such as *always*, *never*, *no one*, *everyone*, *all*, and *none*. When I think or say words like these, I try to check myself because they are usually not true.

## TURNING THE KEY

1. Get a notebook and set aside a few minutes every day to identify false thoughts that are making you anxious or depressed. Then try to think of evidence and reasons to challenge and change these thoughts and replace them with what is true. Maybe ask yourself, "What would I say to a friend who was having these thoughts?" Declare war on your false thoughts and defeat them with true thoughts. Then see how much better you feel.

2. Another way of doing this is to ask yourself these questions and write down the answers:
   - What false thought do you want to change?
   - What are the advantages and disadvantages of believing this false thought?
   - What is an alternative true thought or belief that you could believe?
   - What are the advantages and disadvantages in believing this?
   - Compare the costs and benefits of both the false and the true belief. Which would you prefer to have?

**Write out Philippians 4:8–9. This passage is a bit longer, so if you can't memorize it, just think about it every day for a week.**

_____

_____

_____

_____

**Prayer**

*Lord God of truth, wherever my false thoughts have come from, help me to get rid of them by replacing them with what is true. Help me to find truth about myself to challenge and change my false thoughts. Take away the negativity and make me a more positive person in my thoughts and feelings. Amen.*

# 10

# WORKAHOLIC WILL

I've always loved being busy. I hate sitting around; I get so bored. I much prefer to be active, and I really enjoy my part-time job. I want to be like my dad, someone who's a doer, an achiever, a success.

That's why the past year has been such a nightmare. I would lie in bed but couldn't get my mind to slow down. I wouldn't fall asleep until about two or three in the morning. Then I was exhausted when I got up. I tried to push myself harder to get through my days, but that's not working anymore. I can't sit still and I can't sleep. Even my dad has noticed that things have gotten out of control, but neither of us know what to do. He's arranged for me to see the counselor at my church next week to see if he can help me.

—Will

## The Key of Rest

Will might be the last person you'd think would need a counselor. He's a Type A personality, a leader, a hard worker, and a great example to other kids. I've met many kids like Will. They are part of a hardworking community with a great work ethic. But sometimes a good work ethic can go too far and end up crushing kids. They know how to work hard, but they don't know how to rest hard. When Will sat down with me, I could see he was in a deep hole. He was agitated and couldn't sit still. His knees were bouncing up and down, he was wringing his hands, and he had dark shadows under his eyes.

When I raised the subject of rest, I could see he was cynical. So I started with the Bible's teaching that God has provided the gifts of daily sleep (Psalms 3:5; 4:8; 127:2) and a weekly Sabbath, or rest day (Mark 2:27), to nourish our bodies, minds, and souls. Once I convinced him from the Scriptures, I shared a few articles that showed how even scientists are coming to the same conclusions about the need for daily sleep and a weekly rest day. Then I moved on to the practicalities. How do we make this work?

### SLEEP

Here's what I encouraged Will to do to improve the quantity and quality of his sleep:

- Go to bed and get up at the same time every day. Our bodies love rhythm and regularity.
- At least one hour (preferably two hours) before bedtime, stop studying and using technology. Work, study, and digital media stimulate our minds. This delays sleep, shallows sleep, and shortens sleep.
- Follow the same pre-bed routine every night so that your mind and body know you are heading to bed and begin to produce "sleepy chemicals." That routine might involve eating a light snack, reading a book for pleasure, listening to quiet music, or something else that is calming.
- Don't use your phone as an alarm clock as it will tempt you to look at it last thing before you sleep or first thing in the morning. Get a cheap digital alarm clock, put your phone in another room, and give yourself some peace.
- Pray. Before sleeping, thank God for his help through the day. Look at all the ways he provided and cared for you, and praise him for that. Ask him to calm your mind and heart.

- Be patient. It might take your mind and body a while to adjust to these good sleep habits. But the payoff will be worth it. In a week or so you will begin to fall asleep faster and get a higher quantity and quality of sleep.

Also, if you write your appointments and to-do's down every day in a journal or agenda, you won't lie in bed worrying that you've forgotten something, and you'll fall asleep peacefully.

The first question some counselors ask anxious teens is, "How much sleep are you getting?" That should tell us a lot. The recommended amount of sleep for high schoolers is nine hours a night—ten for middle schoolers!

## SABBATH

Jesus said that God made a weekly Sabbath (or "rest") day for our benefit (Mark. 2:27). It's one of God's great gifts that we should gratefully receive. Using this day as God designed gives us deep, healing rest in a number of ways.

God gives *spiritual rest*. The Lord's Day is a day of gospel rest, a day to remember that salvation is not by our own works but by grace alone. Use the Lord's Day to demonstrate that you have turned away from all your work to rest entirely in Christ's.

God gives *physical rest*. The Sabbath is a day for our bodies to be still, to be renewed by a break from our physical labors. Yes, God calls us to work hard for six days, but he also calls us to rest hard for one day.

God gives *mental rest*. Although our minds are engaged in hearing the word of God and worshiping on the Sabbath, what we do on the Sabbath is such a shift from our usual studies and thought patterns that it becomes a mental rest. Plus, lifting our minds to things above makes things below look much smaller.

God gives us *emotional rest*. Turn off the internet, email, and messaging. Give yourself a total break from digital media one day a week so that you can calm and soothe your frayed emotions. Seek true joy and peace in spiritual things and in renewing the bonds of family and face-to-face friendship.

## Update from Will

I was skeptical when my counselor started talking about more sleep and a weekly day of rest. It made no sense to me. I felt I needed to work harder and more. But I couldn't deny the Bible's teaching, and even science supported it.

So I acted in faith and started taking a whole day off a week on Sunday. I didn't study, and I cut back on using technology and other media that day. Apart from going to church, I chatted with my family, went for a short hike around a nearby lake, read a Christian book, and spent the rest of the time just doing nothing. It was actually quite enjoyable, which surprised me.

I followed my counselor's advice about preparing for sleep the right way. I fell asleep much faster, and awoke refreshed on Monday morning. It's harder to do this on weekdays, but when I get it right, I always sleep better. I'm definitely becoming calmer and happier. My grades have also improved, even though I'm studying less. I like that a lot!

Sometimes I still can't sleep. But my counselor taught me a couple other ways to put myself in a more restful spirit, including breathing exercises and learning to relax my body.

## TURNING THE KEY

You can try the same exercises that Will uses. Of course you can do these when you feel stressed. But you can also get ahead of your anxiety by doing them at set times every day, perhaps associating them with mealtimes or break times.

1. *4 x 4 breathing:* Think of a square, and go around the four sides in these four phases: (1) Breathe in deeply through your nose for four seconds; (2) hold your breath for four; (3) release your breath slowly through your mouth for four seconds; (4) pause for four seconds. Repeat this five to ten times until you feel more relaxed. Our bodies have a nerve that runs through the lungs to the brain, which means that by breathing slowly, messages go to our brain to slow down.

You can also add short prayers to each of these 4 x 4's. For example, (1) Lord Jesus; (2) Give me peace; (3) Holy Spirit; (4) Give me joy.

2. *Body scan:* Scan your body with your mind. Start at your forehead and try to consciously relax the muscles there. Then scan down your face, thinking of your eyes, nose, cheeks, mouth, neck, shoulders, and so on. Pause for a few seconds on each body part, and try to see how much tension you can release from it. Perhaps say, "Let it go." Continue the scan all the way down to your toes. Sometimes it helps to tense up the part of the body you are thinking about, and then let it go.

Before you do each of these exercises, rate your stress on a scale of one to ten. Then do the exercises and notice how the rating goes down. As you do this, you'll see that you do have an element of control over your body and feelings.

**Write out Psalm 46:10 and memorize it.**

_____

_____

_____

_____

**Prayer**

*Great God of rest, thank you for the gift of daily and weekly rest. I confess I have often rejected these good gifts, and I've suffered as a result. Help me restore these healthy habits to my life. And as I learn to relax my body and quiet my mind, help to me to hear your comforting voice in the stillness and silence. Amen.*

# 11

# BEAUTIFUL BRIANNA

I spend a lot of time on my appearance. It's the first thing I think about when I wake up. I have a part-time job, but I'm struggling to save up for a car because I spend all my money on new clothes and makeup.

I'm always fighting with my mom because she says my jeans are too tight, my tops are too low, my shorts are too short, and so on. It's so stressful.

My friends say I'm gorgeous, and I get a lot of attention from the boys, but I'm not happy with myself. I can put on a smile when I'm with people and act confidently, but deep down I don't think I'll ever be pretty enough.

—Brianna

## The Key of Identity

What's the first word that comes to mind when you think about yourself? What do you answer when you ask yourself, "Who am I?" This can be difficult to answer in our teen years because these are often times of great change and confusion as we transition from childhood to adulthood. Like Brianna, we can end up adopting a false and harmful identity. Here are some common examples:

*I am my body.* Do you define yourself by your body, like Brianna did? Nine out of ten girls are unhappy with their body. "I'm fat . . . skinny . . . tall . . . small . . . ugly . . . beautiful . . ."

*I am my grades.* Do you get your sense of worth from your performance at school? If you get good grades, you feel good about yourself and look down on others. If you get bad grades, you are a failure, and are jealous of others.

*I am my friends.* Do you build your identity around having friends—online or real life? The more friends you have, the better you feel. Or is your life worthless unless you have a boyfriend or girlfriend?

*I am my sin.* Is there a sin in your life that dominates your thinking? You cannot think about yourself without thinking of that sin, that habit, that incident.

*I am my sport.* If you win, or your team wins, you feel great. If not, life's not worth living. Your mood depends on medals and trophies.

*I am my anxiety/depression.* Have you let your anxiety or depression define you? When you look at yourself, all you see is depression or anxiety.

*I am my past.* Maybe you've been the victim of abuse. I'm so sorry. It was not your fault. It should not have happened to you. It was wrong. But are you allowing that abuse to ruin the rest of your life by letting it dominate your thoughts and define who you are?

*I am my sexual desires.* God created us so that sexual desire, intimacy, and enjoyment would be part of human experience. Sin, however, has distorted this good gift, with the result that what God designed to be a part of us can become the whole of us. We're especially vulnerable to this in our teen years when we experience the awakening of sexual desire. This can become so powerful that we allow it to define us at times. However, it's a big mistake to let extreme, confusing, and temporary emotions define us for the rest of our lives.

What's so bad about all these identities? Some are simply false; they just aren't true. Others are based on factors that are constantly changing. Some of them give power to other people to define us. Others are given first place when they don't deserve even tenth place. And all of this creates a lot of mental and emotional distress.

So we're going to replace these false and shaky identities with a true and strong identity, one given to us by the God who made us and knows us best. We do this in four steps.

### STEP ONE: I AM AN IMAGE BEARER OF GOD

God made you to bear his image (Gen. 1:27), to show who he is to the rest of the world. That's your fundamental identity and purpose. Therefore, before you even answer "Who am I?," you need to find out who God is. Often we go wrong on the "Who am I?" question because we've got the wrong answer to the "Who is God?" question.

### STEP TWO: I AM A SINNER

Although God originally made us to carry and show his image to the world, we are now sinners and our sin has distorted that image. That's why we need the Bible. It shows us who God is and who we are.

### STEP THREE: I AM A CHRISTIAN

To fully recover your God-given identity and replace all false identities, you need to become a Christian through faith in Christ. Faith in Christ gives you a new identity in Christ. Think of all that becomes true of you when you can truly say, "I am a Christian."

*I am loved by God.* God has loved me from eternity past and will love me forever (Jeremiah 31:3). Therefore, whoever else loves me or doesn't love me matters much less.

*I am a child of God.* It doesn't matter who my natural family is if I am a child of God. As part of God's family, I need never be lonely because I have brothers and sisters all over the world (Romans 8:14–17).

*I am accepted by God.* Others may be cast out and reject me, but God accepts me 100 percent (Romans 15:7).

*I am forgiven by God.* Yes, I am a sinner, and I have committed terrible sins, but Christ's blood washes and cleanses me from all sin and makes me clean in his sight. I am white as snow (Isaiah 1:18).

*I am the body of Christ.* If my body is a member of Christ's body, what more can I ask for? It may not be the most attractive or desirable body to others, but Christ has shed his blood to make my body part of his body (1 Corinthians 6:15).

*I am a joy to God.* God doesn't just tolerate me; he enjoys me and sings songs over me and about me (Zephaniah 3:17).

None of these things ever change if you are a Christian. They don't depend on your feelings or on other people. You are not defined by your body, your grades, your friends, your enemies, your sin, your sports, your successes, your failures, or your sexuality. You are defined by God, and with this God-given identity in hand you can defy every other attempt to define or identify you. Let God's voice silence all the other voices.

If you are not a Christian yet, I hope you will read about this incredible identity and say, "I want that for myself."

**STEP FOUR: I AM UNIQUE**

Steps one through three are equally true of all God's children. However, that doesn't mean that God just turns out Christian clones, look-alikes in every respect. No, God has made each of us different with unique personalities, characters, gifts, graces, and callings.

We make a big mistake if we make our uniqueness the most important thing about us. However, we also err if we ignore or downplay our God-given uniqueness. That's why we come to God and ask him—not our parents, our culture, or our friends— "Who do you want me to be?" If we answer this right, so much else will be right.

---

### Update from Brianna

I was definitely defining myself by my looks. My identity was tied up with my body. Through counseling, I came to see that this was causing me to be depressed. I could never be beautiful enough. There were always going to be lots of girls prettier than me.

Once my counselor introduced me to the four steps, I had a plan to recover my stolen identity and replace my false identity. I thought this would work quicker than it did, but it's taking time because I had embraced a false identity for so long. I do have more good days than bad days though, especially when I consciously work through the four steps.

The key thing has been to get my identity from God, not from my body, not from my looks, and not from other people. I don't think so much about how I look now, and I'm happier. I spend a lot less money on clothes and makeup. I might even save up enough money for a car by next summer.

## TURNING THE KEY

1. Write down what first comes to mind when you ask, "Who am I?" What words do you first think of?
2. Ask yourself where these words are coming from. Where are you getting your identity from?
3. Rebuild your identity using the four steps.

**Write out the first part of 1 Corinthians 15:10 and memorize it.**

_____

_____

_____

_____

**Prayer**

*Lord, I confess that I let others define me. I confess that I have had many false identities. I want to be defined by you. Enable me to get my identity from you and to rejoice in it. When others try to steal my God-given identity and replace it, help me to fight for truth and say, "No, by the grace of God, I am what I am." Amen.*

# 12

# MEDIA MAX

A few weeks ago, a guy spoke to our youth group at church about the dangers of overusing digital technology. I'd heard it all before, and I was planning to tune out and goof off with my friends in the back row. But the speaker brought a lot of scientific research, which caught my attention. In his first talk, he showed how the latest science had found that technology was damaging young brains and also causing a lot of emotional problems. But it was the brain thing that really worried me, especially because it rang true.

I've felt for a while that my brain is getting fried with nonstop texts, emails, notifications, video games, YouTube videos, movies, and other things I don't want to talk about. But I hadn't realized that this was actually changing and harming my brain. I know I've got to get this under control. It's not just that I want to do well at school and go to college; I also want to be happier. I'm hyper all the time. I'm never at peace.

—*Max*

## The Key of Digital Detox

I was that speaker, and I am convinced—from scientific research, from personal experience, and from counseling teens—that any attempt to replace anxiety and depression with peace and joy must have a plan for getting our digital devices and social media under control. All the research indicates that our overuse and misuse of digital technology is one of the greatest causes of mental and emotional distress today, especially among teens.

Science shows that overuse of digital technology reduces attention spans, concentration, reasoning skills, IQ, brain density, emotional resilience, and the length and quality of our sleep. Also, excessive use of social media has been connected with poor self-esteem, social isolation, negative self-comparison (often called "compare and despair"), feelings of inadequacy, the pursuit of perfectionism, and shallow relationships.[1]

Most social media platforms actually make anxiety worse, and Instagram is by far the worst culprit.[2] We were never intended to know so much about other people. Especially when we are young, our minds need to focus on developing and growing and living—not on other people's lives or problems we can't fix.

Sexting and pornography bring burdens of guilt, shame, and anxiety. Images of violence leave their own scars on our brains and psyche.

Even when we admit that damage is occurring, it's very difficult to get technology and social media under control. That's why our overuse of it is increasingly being compared to an addiction, with brain scans showing that screen time affects the brain in exactly the same way that cocaine does. Some researchers are even calling screens "electronic cocaine" and "digital heroin." This is why we need a digital detox.

## DIGITAL DETOX

You can do a digital detox by doing three things. (I'll refer to phones but these apply to all digital devices, including game consoles.)

- *Reduce frequency:* limit the number of times you check your phone.

1. Jean Twenge, *iGen: Why Today's Super-Connected Kids Are Growing Up Less Rebellious, More Tolerant, Less Happy—and Completely Unprepared for Adulthood—and What That Means for the Rest of Us* (New York: Atria, 2017).
2. Amanda Macmillan, "Why Instagram Is the Worst Social Media for Mental Health," *Time*, May 25, 2017, https://time.com/4793331/instagram-social-media-mental-health/.

• *Reduce duration:* shorten how long you spend on your phone.
• *Reduce damage:* stop exposure to damaging content.

Here are some specific tips for implementing a digital detox. *Start the day with God.* Do not check your phone before you check in with God by reading his word and praying. Do not let your phone interrupt you during this time. Ideally, put it on airplane mode or put it in another room. Let the first impressions made on your mind each day be from heaven.

*Turn off notifications.* Your brain needs peace and quiet. It needs to rest regularly throughout the day. So why not carve out times when you simply turn off all the beeps and buzzes and pings? Start with one hour a day, and then increase that hour or add more hours scattered throughout the day.

*Limit your check-ins to once an hour.* Many teens check their phones over thirty times an hour. Commit to checking in only once or twice every hour. Few messages require an instant reply. Try to view your phone as a person. Would you let a person constantly interrupt you throughout the day when you were doing other important things or in conversations? No, you would tell people they were rude and stop them. Do the same with your phone.

*Put your phone in another room when you are studying.* That way, you not only won't be interrupted but you also won't be tempted to reach for it and be distracted from your studies. This will increase the quality of study time and free up time for other activities.

*Inform your friends.* Tell them what you are doing to limit your tech use so that they will not expect instant answers to texts. Suggest putting your phones off or away when you are hanging out.

*Avoid reading terrible news.* Don't let your phone become a portable bad-news machine. You can read the headlines, but try to minimize exposure to violent stories and images.

*Consume true, good, and beautiful media.* Fill your mind and heart with healthy, fun, beautiful, and truthful media to replace the opposite (Philippians 4:8). That rules out many computer games.

*Cut out pre-bed use of your phone.* Using screens right before bed not only introduces things to worry about into our minds, but it also delays, interrupts, and shortens sleep.

*Ask for help.* You need accountability and support, so why not ask your parents to help you get technology under control? Use Covenant Eyes to keep you accountable (see www.covenant eyes.com). Perhaps designate an area in the living room or kitchen where you have to leave your phone when at home. If you are being bullied, sexted, or being asked to send nudes to people, you need to tell your parents or a teacher and ask them for help.

*Enjoy the moment.* Put the phone away and enjoy the scenery, the event, or the friends without having to Snapchat or Instagram it all.

*Build real-world face-to-face relationships.* Spend more time with people than with your phone. Do things together in the real world, especially sports, hobbies, and simply relaxing and enjoying one another.

All the scientific research encourages us that if we can get digital technology under control, we will do so much better—physically, intellectually, relationally, vocationally, educationally, financially, emotionally, and spiritually.

---

### Update from Max

This might be a lifelong struggle for me, but I know the fight will be worth it. When I completed the digital detox questionnaire (see below), I was shocked. But I shouldn't have been. In my heart, I knew that a lot of my problems stemmed from misusing technology. I didn't admit it before, but I was feeling really guilty about the porn I was watching too.

The practical advice in the digital detox has helped me to get technology under control and reduce the hyperstimulation of my brain. I've still got a lot of work to do here, but I've made a good start. A lot of my friends don't understand, but I know I have got to stick with it.

Perhaps the biggest help has been this verse from Scripture: "Every good gift and every perfect gift is from above, coming down from the Father of lights" (James 1:17). Now, whenever I'm tempted to abuse or overuse technology, I say to myself, "My loving heavenly Father gave me this good gift, so how dare I turn that against him and myself?"

## TURNING THE KEY

I've given you many practical tips already in this chapter. Now let me point you to an additional resource Max mentioned that will help you implement a digital detox.

1. Go to www.whyamIfeelinglikethis.com/digitaldetox and complete the digital detox questionnaire to find out how digitally intoxicated you are. The site will also highlight areas to work on to bring down your score.
2. Fill this out once a week for a month in order to track your progress. You'll find that even just building awareness of how you use digital technology will reduce its place in your life and improve your health in every way.

**Write out James 1:17 and memorize it.**

_____

_____

_____

_____

**Prayer**

*Giver of every good and perfect gift, I confess that I have overused and misused your gift of digital technology. Use this digital detox to help me use your gift in a way that pleases you and that makes it a source of peace and joy rather than of anxiety and depression. Amen.*

# 13

# FRIENDLY FIONA

Friends have always been important to me. In fact, friendship is all I think about. Getting friends, keeping friends, pleasing friends. It makes me so anxious. I'm always worried about what my friends think about me. After being with a friend, I go over everything in my mind. Did I say the right thing? Did I do the right thing? What does she think about me now? When I buy clothes, or makeup, or get my hair done, I'm always thinking, "What will my friends say?"

Recently, I started a relationship with a senior boy (that's the grade above me). He's good-looking, and my friends are jealous. He wants to move beyond just kissing. Last week he asked me to send him nudes. I didn't want to lose him, so I kind of did. I didn't show everything, though. But now the boys at school are sharing my picture, laughing at me, and calling me a slut. The other girls won't talk to me, even though they do this too. I want to die.

—*Fiona*

## The Key of Christ's Friendship

As Fiona's story illustrates, friendships can create a lot of angst in our teen years. We might lack friends, struggle to make friends, lose friends, and experience ongoing drama and shifting alliances. On top of all that, there's the added strain that comes from friendships with the opposite sex. That's a lot of stress, isn't it? How can we possibly be happy when all this is going on?

Fiona shared her story with Kathy, her mentor at church. Kathy recently graduated from college and is a strong Christian. A couple of years ago, she started meeting Fiona for coffee every month or so, and they text almost every day. Kathy had watched Fiona become more and more obsessed with friends and saw that it was making her miserable.

They had many conversations in the following weeks. They talked through how to create and cultivate healthy relationships, and how to keep them in the right place. Kathy encouraged Fiona to prioritize the friendship of Jesus and then let that friendship influence all other friendships. Kathy summarizes her time with Fiona in the following.

### JESUS IS YOUR BEST FRIEND

I felt so sorry for Fiona. I knew what she was going through. I saw a lot of my younger self in her. What changed my life was when I finally realized that while friends are important, friendship with Jesus Christ is most important. If Jesus is our best friend, then we have the best friend in all the world. I knew that if Fiona got this, it would impact all her relationships for the better.

Our conversations were messy, but here's the tidy version of all that we discussed. I started by showing how wonderful a friend Jesus is, and then we talked about how friendship with Jesus changes all other friendships.

Jesus is a *surprising* friend. You might think you are the last person Jesus would want as a friend. That's what many people said of Jesus's choice of friends (Matthew 9:11), but that didn't put him off. In fact, he loves to pick the most surprising of friends.

Jesus is the *perfect* friend because no one can love us more or do more for his friends than he does. He came to this world and laid down his life for his friends (John 15:13).

He is a *loyal* friend. He is always there, he will never give up on us, he will never disappoint us, he will never betray us, and he will never leave us (Hebrews 13:5).

He is a *close* friend. We can talk to him by prayer wherever we are. By reading his word, we can hear his voice speaking into our lives whenever we want.

What a friend we have in Jesus! There is no better friend of sinners (Luke 15:1–2). But, as I emphasized to Fiona, that friendship has consequences.

### IF JESUS IS YOUR BEST FRIEND . . .

*You will not idolize other friends.* While friendships with our peers are valuable, they don't come close to the value of Christ's friendship. If Christ is my best friend, then I won't make friendship with anyone else a god, something I must have.

*You will be other-centered.* Christ sought out friendships, not so much for his own benefit but for the benefit of those he befriended. He cared not about what he could get out of a relationship but what he could give to a relationship. Much friendship stress comes from trying to attain a status through our friendships. Christ, though, reached down in his friendships.

*You will find sympathy when friends disappoint.* Christ's best friends disappointed throughout his life and especially at his death, when one betrayed him, one denied him, and all forsook him and fled (Mark 14:50). He knows loneliness, betrayal, and abandonment and can therefore sympathize with you.

*You will have a small circle of close friends.* Christ did not have the same friendships with everyone. He had twelve friends, three close friends (Peter, James, and John), and one best friend (John). Sometimes friendship angst comes from trying to have too many friends. If we have one best friend, a few close friends, and a wider circle of not-so-close friends, we are doing really well.

*You will not be possessive about your friends.* Jesus was also comfortable with his friends being friends with others. He was not jealous of them having other friends in their lives.

*You will seek a boyfriend or girlfriend who loves Jesus.* When we are old enough, and we begin to think about this, our first question should be, "Does he or she love Jesus?" We will not want to enter into the closest possible human friendship with someone who does not love our best friend, Jesus Christ.

*You will draw physical boundaries.* Jesus said that we are his friends if we do whatever he has commanded us (John 15:14). Jesus made very clear that sexual contact outside of marriage is sinful, as is even looking on someone with sexual desire (Matt. 5:27–28). Therefore, if we don't want to damage our friendship with Jesus or our friendship with our boyfriend or girlfriend, we will have clear boundaries that we will not cross. This includes not only physical touching but sharing photos. If you wouldn't let someone touch you there, you shouldn't be asking for or sharing photos of it.

There should be no touching of private parts (the areas we cover with our underwear) until marriage. That's when private parts are no longer one's personal private property but become shared. When we start touching one another in areas that God has forbidden, we open a whole new dimension of complicated emotions and stress. This will usually damage the relationship with one another and, potentially, with Jesus.

That's a quick version of many hours of conversations with Fiona (and many cups of coffee).

---

### Update from Fiona

Kathy has helped me so much. I eventually saw how friends had become my idol and my identity. When the inner chatter starts up about what my friends think about me, I tell myself that Jesus is my best friend and my identity. He defines my life, not my friends.

Once I got that, it was easier to end my relationship with my boyfriend. I still cried, but I knew it was the right thing to do. In fact, I've decided to wait until after high school to think about having a boyfriend. I think it will save me a lot of stress in the meantime.

There's still a lot of drama in my friend circles, and I still have my ups and downs. But the ups are not so high and the downs are not so low if I keep Jesus number one in my life. I've still got a lot of work to do, but Kathy is patient and always there to help me through the crises by getting my focus back on Jesus.

## TURNING THE KEY

The next time you have friend drama, come back to Kathy's advice and write out a few ways it can help you in your situation.

**Write out John 15:13 and memorize it.**

_____

_____

_____

_____

**Prayer**

*Jesus, although I don't deserve this, be my best friend, and show me how to make your friendship the most important friendship in the world. Bless me with a few good friends and make me a good friend to others by being willing to suffer and sacrifice for the good of others as you did. Amen.*

# 14

# BULLIED BENTON

I've been bullied a lot at school in the past year. It's mainly one guy, but his friends join in too. It's mainly verbal, but they do threaten me at times and push me around in the hallways. I've tried to avoid them by not going to the bathroom or the dining hall, but now they wait for me at the school gates. I've been skipping school, and my teachers have noticed my grades going down. My guidance counselor asked me what's wrong, but I couldn't tell him. I haven't told my parents either, but I know they're worried about me.

Last week the main bully got my cell number and started sending me scary messages and horrible pictures, often late at night. I have terrible nightmares, and sometimes I wake up in a sweat. I now jump and start shaking when my phone pings.

—Benton

## The Key of Protection

Post-traumatic stress disorder (PTSD) is what soldiers sometimes suffer from when they come back from a fierce battle. The memory of what they saw and heard is so disturbing that it causes anxiety and depression. The only war zone Benton has been in is the schoolyard. Yet the verbal and physical abuse he's suffered there at the hands of bullies has left him as traumatized as any soldier facing the Taliban. His fight-or-flight system is always on.

Benton is not alone. Every day one hundred and sixty thousand kids skip school to avoid bullying, with 20 percent of students being bullied every year.[1] Bullying is one of the major causes of depression and anxiety in teens, and it's one of the hardest problems to deal with. So what can we do? How can we help Benton and others like him?

### LOOK IN THE MIRROR

I was bullied at school. I was spat on, humiliated, shoved, laughed at, and lied about. I was physically attacked numerous times. My twin brother was not as fast a runner as I was, and he ended up in the hospital for days after being attacked by a dozen or so teens at a train station.

I sometimes stayed away from school or left school early to avoid gangs that would gather at the school gates. I remember looking out the windows during English class one day and seeing about fifteen older teens with sticks and chains shouting at me and two of my friends that they were going to kill us.

Although sometimes people hate us without any good reason, I have to admit that I gave some boys a reason to hate me and attack me. I had a big mouth, and I said things about them or to them that annoyed them. Although they were totally wrong to bully me, I didn't help the situation. We can admit that and still seek outside help, though, as I did. God hates all abuse, wants it stopped, and the bullies punished. So don't use your own faults to stop you asking for adult intervention.

### LOOK TO GOD

Ask God for confidence and strength to trust him. Bullies love fear, but God can take away or reduce our fear. He can help us to project trust and confidence in him. Bullies enjoy making us sad, angry, or scared. If, with the Lord's help, you can show you are none of these things, they will often lose interest.

---

1. The 2017 School Crime Supplement (National Center for Education Statistics and Bureau of Justice) indicates that, nationwide, about 20 percent of students ages twelve to eighteen experienced bullying.

Also, ask God for wisdom to know how to walk away or to avoid certain situations. That may involve sitting at a different desk, avoiding certain places, or walking home a different way.

If you are trapped by a bully, ask God to protect you, then say with a clear calm voice, "Please get out of the way. I'm leaving now. Do not do this again." If necessary, put your arms in front of your face with your palms facing outward. If you are being attacked, cry loudly to God for help and also for someone to come and help you.

## LOOK TO OTHERS

God has appointed leaders to protect the innocent and punish evildoers (Romans 13:1–4). He hates bullying and calls parents, teachers, pastors, and police to protect the weak and punish bullies. Your guidance counselor has probably been trained to deal with bullying and will know how to protect you. Sometimes we can ask friends or other bystanders to help us as well.

## LOOK AWAY

When I was a teen, I got away from bullies when I got home. Things are different now because bullies can follow us into our homes via our phones and other digital devices. But we still have the power to limit their access to us. We can stop looking at our devices. We can put blocks on phone numbers. We can delete apps. Yes, we will miss out on some things, but we will get relief as well. Try to make your home and bedroom a peace zone not a war zone.

## LOOK AT CHRIST

Jesus Christ was bullied by more people and in more ways than we ever were or will be. He was bullied by politicians, soldiers, judges, religious leaders, mobs, and even by the devil and his armies. He knows the physical, mental, and emotional pain of being bullied. We might think, "No one understands!" but he does (Hebrews 4:15).

But Christ is not just a sympathizer; he's also a model and example for us when we are bullied. The apostle Peter saw Christ being bullied close up and recorded how he responded (1 Peter 2:20–25). He was patient (v. 20), he didn't retaliate (v. 22), he trusted God to look after him and put things right (v. 23), and even loved his enemies (vv. 24–25). None of this is easy, but Christ calls us to copy his model response. This doesn't mean that we simply passively take whatever people say or do against us. For example, in Luke 4:30, Jesus found a way to escape from bullies. Romans 13 also tells us that God has provided authorities like the police and other authority figures to punish evildoers and protect the innocent. But it does call us to a humble Christlike spirit as we respond to bullying.

## LOOK OUT FOR OTHERS

Maybe you're not being bullied right now, but others are. Look out for them and offer them friendship and support. Be like Christ to them and show them his character.

### Update from Benton

Things are quite a bit better. I eventually told my guidance counselor about the bullying, and he got my parents to come to a meeting. Just telling someone was a relief. When my dad heard, he wanted to go straight to the bully's parents or the police. But my guidance counselor wants to do things more slowly and gradually. I know he's got my back, and he's looking out for me. I don't know all he's doing in the background, but it seems to be working.

I got a new phone, so the bullies can't get at me when I'm home. I'm not skipping school anymore, but I go out a different gate and go home another way. Prayer has helped me a lot. My dad and I read the Bible and pray together before school each day. When I get home, I thank God for a peaceful day. This whole experience has taught me a lot about Jesus's suffering, and also made me more sensitive to the suffering of others.

## TURNING THE KEY

In the parent's guide (*Why Is My Teenager Feeling Like This?*) I've outlined a number of ways that adults can help you if you are being bullied. Here are some steps to handle cyberbullying.

1. *Talk.* Tell your parents or a teacher. Reach out to someone you trust and tell him or her what's happening, how it started, and who is involved. Adults can help you make a plan to deal with the bullying.
2. *Document.* Keep a record via screenshots of what's been posted.
3. *Block.* Block people from texting, messaging you, or following you on social media. Use privacy settings on social media to control who sees what. Also, do not share your passwords with any other kids.
4. *Report.* An adult can get in touch with the social media platform to get their help. If the bullying does not stop and physical threats are made, you should ask the police for advice.
5. *Remember.* Remind yourself that most people bully because they have something sad or bad in their background. As it is often said, "Hurt people hurt people."
6. *Pray.* Pray for God's protection. Pray for God to change the bully's heart.

**Write out 1 Peter 2:23 and memorize it.**

_____

_____

_____

_____

**Prayer**

*Lord Jesus, you know I'm being bullied and how scared and de-pressed I am. You also know what it's like to be bullied. Because you are the Judge, I commit myself to you to protect me and punish evildoers. Guide me also in my reactions to bullies so that I am Christlike. Give my parents and teachers wisdom and courage to act as your representatives on earth. And through it all give me a heart to help the bullied. Amen.*

# 15

# REBELLIOUS ROB

I have the worst parents in the world. They are far stricter than all my friends' parents. They don't listen to me, and they don't understand me. It makes me so angry. We fight all the time over everything: where I go, who I'm with, what time I'm home, and on and on. I'm always getting grounded or fined—or they take my phone away. I really hate them at times. I wish I had parents like my friends do. It's depressing. They want me to see a counselor, but they're the ones that have a problem, not me.

—Rob

## The Key of Respect

Our relationship with our parents changes a lot during our teen years. We are no longer children, totally dependent on our father and mother for everything; but neither are we yet independent adults. We are developing our own personalities, opinions, and choices. But these often conflict with our parents' views of who we should be, what we should think, and what we should choose. All this change creates varying degrees of tension in our relationships with our parents during the teen years.

How do we navigate these stress points in a way that honors our parents as God commands (Exodus 20:12; Ephesians 6:2) and therefore reduce the tension that results in so much anxiety and depression? That's the question Rob's counselor focused on, and over a number of sessions offered the following advice and direction.

## PRAY

Your parents are not perfect but they are usually trying their best to please God and do you good. Ask God to give them wisdom to be godly parents, to give you good guidance in the teen years. Pray also for yourself, that you would know how to love and respect them even in areas where you may disagree. If your parents are not Christians, pray that they would hear the gospel of Jesus Christ and be saved.

## HONOR

Try to speak well of your parents and to them, even when they may be wrong. Joseph and Mary rebuked the twelve-year-old Jesus because they did not know where he was. Although he was doing nothing wrong, and indeed was doing the will of his heavenly Father, Jesus submitted to them and went home with them (Luke 2:51).

Even if we strongly disagree with our parents, they are God's representatives in our lives and, therefore, we honor him by honoring them. That means listening to them carefully and giving their words thoughtful consideration rather than automatically rejecting them.

## PAUSE

The best way to avoid speaking in a way you will later regret is to pause before speaking. Count to ten and breathe deep and slow when you feel your anger rising. If that doesn't calm you down, ask for a few minutes or even an hour to think about what your parents have said. Then pray about it, asking God for help to see your parents' point of view and for help to agree or disagree in a Christlike way.

## COMMUNICATE

If lashing out is one extreme, the other is bottling things up. That's when we internalize our frustration. We try to hide it or we make it obvious that we are angry by silence, facial expressions, or withdrawal. Flaming out against our parents burns them, but bottling it up starts an internal fire that burns ourselves. Instead of lashing out or bottling up, we need to learn how to express our opinions calmly and peaceably. This is also far more likely to succeed. And do all this face-to-face rather than over text.

## NEGOTIATE

When we disagree over things like bedtimes or tech use or being allowed to go to certain places, we might want to try to meet our parents at some point in between. If they insist that we only spend one hour a day online, and we want to spend two hours, maybe there's a point in between that everyone could live with. Oftentimes we can find solutions by listening to one another and adjusting accordingly.

## CONFESS

If we sin against our parents, it's important to confess that and seek their forgiveness. Don't say, "I'm sorry if I hurt you. . . ." Say, "I'm sorry I did wrong (or said wrong), and I know that was hurtful to you. Please forgive me." Give them time to accept your confession and grant forgiveness. Remember, even if they forgive us, they may have to discipline us to teach us how serious sin is so that we don't repeat it.

What if our parents have wronged us or made a mistake? And they will, because they are not perfect! If they admit the wrong and ask for our forgiveness, we must give it, and then forget it (Matthew 6:14–15).

If they do wrong but don't ask for forgiveness, then we must leave it to God to put right (Romans 12:19). Picture yourself releasing the wrong to God, and say to him: "I give this wrong to you, Lord, and trust you to do right and put things right in the right time."

## INVEST

Many of the conflicts with our parents would be avoided or would not be so drama-filled if we simply spent more time with them. Sometimes we hardly know our parents because we are so busy with friends, studies, sports, social media, and work.

Take time to invest in your parents' lives. Sit down with them, and ask them about their day. Show an interest in them as people, and grow in love toward them. Ask them for help or advice. Offer to help them with housework or yard work. Investing time, energy, and attention in this relationship will prevent many potential disagreements and make them easier to manage when they do arise.

## ONE-SIDED?

"But this is all one-sided!" you complain. Don't worry, in the parent's guide, I've given your dad and mom a number of areas to work on too. With both sides working on their responsibilities, hopefully we can make this relationship a source of peace and joy rather than further anxiety and depression.

--- **Update from Rob** ---

I didn't want to see a counselor, partly because I thought the problem was all on my parents' side. I still think they've got to change, but I realize now that I have to change too. Also, I wasn't aware of how depressed I had become, and how that was distorting my thinking and feeling. Being so angry all the time was really getting me down.

My parents have started reading *Why Is My Teenager Feeling Like This? A Guide for Helping Teens through Anxiety and Depression*, and I see that they are making a bigger effort to listen to me and reason with me rather than treating me like a child. We've talked through issues from the past, and we've all apologized for different things and tried to forgive one another.

We still have arguments but we no longer fight. Our relationship is calmer, and we're more respectful of one another. We are all praying more for one another, and I would say that I love my parents more now. I do feel a lot better about myself; I'm happier and more peaceful.

## TURNING THE KEY

As prevention is better than cure, we want to put some steps in place that will reduce the number and intensity of conflicts we have with our parents.

1. Once your parents have read their book, come together and talk about ways you can improve your relationship with them so that it becomes a source of peace rather than stress.
2. Meet with your parents to talk through which of these models you will use in conflict situations (Hint: only the last two are biblical).
   - *The bulldozer:* You confront every wrong and run everyone over.
   - *The doormat:* You never confront wrong but let everyone run over you.
   - *The doormat with spikes:* You don't confront people when they've done wrong, but you try to damage them in more subtle ways (e.g., gossip, silent treatement).
   - *The pillar:* You stand up for yourself but in a way that doesn't damage other people. You are assertive but not aggressive. You are strong but not attacking.
   - *Aikido:* This is a martial art that people use to defend themselves while also protecting their attacker from injury. You might call it strategic side-stepping. If it's a small matter, you say, "I'm not going to let this get to me; I choose to let it go."[1]

If neither of your parents are Christians, you are still to respect and pray for them. You can do what God requires you to do even if they don't.

---

1. See Lisa Damour, *Under Pressure* (New York: Random House, 2018), 80–81.

**Write out Colossians 3:13 and memorize it.**

_____

_____

_____

_____

**Prayer**

*Thank you, Lord, for my parents. I'm sorry I have sometimes disrespected them, which has caused us all a lot of stress and anger. As I ask for your forgiveness, help me to ask for their forgiveness when needed, and help me to give forgiveness when they need it too. Change me into a peacemaker, and help us all to navigate conflict and disagreement in ways that respect each other and above all honor you. Amen.*

# 16

# PERFECT PEYTON

My parents are very successful, and they want the same for me. Both my dad and mom have great jobs and are well-respected in our church and community. I love them, and I want to do them proud, but I don't think I can live up to their expectations. I'm not as clever or sporty as my older brother and sister, who both went to great colleges, and the pressure is really getting to me. Every day feels like I am on trial. I try my hardest, but it's never enough. I'm so afraid of making a mistake. My teachers and soccer coach also point to my sister's success, which just increases my anxiety. I recently tried to relieve the pressure by cutting myself, which helped for a few minutes, but then made me feel even worse.

—*Peyton*

## The Key of Realistic Expectations

Just as Rob's rebellion against his parents caused him anxiety and depression, so, too, is Peyton's desire to please her parents. Unrealistic expectations can stir up a ton of worry and anxiety. It may be our own expectation of ourselves, or it may be those of our teachers, coach, church, parents, boss, or even cultural expectations. Let's look at how to reduce the pressure that accompanies expectations of perfection or the terror of imperfection.

## HIGH EXPECTATIONS

It's part of human nature to have aims and ambitions. God commanded humanity to grow, expand, flourish, and make the most of this world and our talents (Genesis 1:28; 9:1; Matthew 13:1–23; John 15:8). God does not expect us to be static, stagnant, or slothful. Rather, the Bible commands hard work and encourages progress. Problems arise when the pressure of expectation is too much, lasts too long, sets too high a standard, or is applied to too many areas of life.

## IMPOSSIBLE EXPECTATIONS

We live in a culture of impossible expectations. Teens like Peyton are under incredible pressure to succeed on a number of fronts, including school, sports, church, work, and friends. Young people face constant testing, quizzing, examining, and ranking. To top it off, social media communicates unreasonable expectations. We see the best photos of the best moments presented by the best kids in the best possible way, and we feel the pressure to match up. "If everyone else looks like this or lives like this, so should I!" We then add our own expectations to everyone else's. All these impossible expectations lead to an inevitable sense of failure and shame.

## REALISTIC EXPECTATIONS

So how do we aim high without aiming impossibly high? How do we set realistic expectations?

*Ask God for your life purpose.* God has a purpose for your life, a purpose that he has designed to fit your particular talents, passions, and strengths. It's vital that you discover this by prayer and study of God's word. Ask him, "Lord, how have you gifted me, and what will you have me to do? What passions and strengths have you given me?" If we can get clarity about *God's* expectations of us, then we can put everyone else's expectations in the right place.

*Get the basics in place.* If you can't take a weekly day off, if you can't get eight hours of sleep a night, and if you can't exercise daily, then you're doing too much. Get these basics of life in place, and whatever time is left is the time you have to do whatever God calls you to do.

*Prioritize and prune.* You cannot do everything, and God doesn't want you to try. List your aims in order of importance and chop off the bottom one or two. List your responsibilities and chop off the bottom couple. Notice what didn't happen. The world did not stop, nor did your life fall apart. Notice what has happened. You've created a little bit of margin, some white space in your mind and life. How much better you will feel!

*Cut back on social media.* Most of the images you see on social media are not realistic depictions of life. They are carefully posed and curated snapshots that convey a false message. The reality of our friends' lives is usually very different. So why put yourself through so much unnecessary torture by filling your mind with what is artificial?

*Accept our limitations.* God has given different talents and different amounts of each talent to different people. No two people are the same. God does not call a five-talent person to be a ten-talent person. He calls the five-talent person to use the five talents well.

*Learn to say no.* Perhaps you think that you can't say no to other people without harming them or your relationship. Try saying this the next time a friend asks you to go somewhere you don't want to go: "I'm really sorry, I can't make that work. But how about we meet up tomorrow evening for coffee?" You're saying no without going into all the reasons, but you're also showing that you still want to be friends.

*Have an audience of one.* Ask yourself, "How would my priorities and choices change if Christ were the only observer here?" (see Col. 3:23). Our working and striving change when we are doing it for Christ rather than for ourselves or anyone else.

*Trust in Christ's perfection.* There was only one perfect person, Jesus Christ, and any attempt to achieve personal perfection is an attempt to manage without him. Let his perfection cover your imperfection. Speaking of which . . .

## FAILED EXPECTATIONS

*Failure is inevitable.* It doesn't matter how clever you are, one day you are going to fail. You may fail to get into your preferred college. You might fail an exam. You will fail at something. Everyone does at some point.

*Failure is not the worst thing that can happen to you.* The most gifted students are usually the most anxious about failing. But there are some important lessons you cannot learn without failing. Failure is an opportunity for growth, not least in humility. Failure teaches us our limitations and weaknesses.

*Failing in one area does not make us a total failure.* There is a big difference between saying "I failed" and "I am a failure." Saying "I failed" means we are not defined by our failure. Failure then does not determine or ruin our whole lives. Say, "I made a mistake" not, "I am a mistake."

*Failing will soon be forgotten.* If you mess up or say something you regret, ask yourself, "How important will this be in a day, in a week, in a month, in a year, in ten years?" This will give you some perspective.

*Failure redirects our lives.* I can look back on some of my failures with gratitude because I can see how God used them to redirect my life. If I had succeeded, I might have ended up in a terrible marriage or a morally compromised job. Through my failure, God closed a door in order to open a better door. I've also seen smaller failures prevent bigger ones.

---

### Update from Peyton

The most healing words in my recovery have been Jesus's words to the woman who poured oil on his feet. My pastor preached on this a few weeks ago, and pointed out how, when others criticized this as wasteful, Jesus replied, "Leave her alone. Why do you trouble her? . . . She has done what she could" (Mark 14:6, 8).

I repeat these last words often to myself now: "She has done what she could." When perfectionism and unrealistic expectations raise their ugly heads and whisper, "You're not good enough. You haven't done enough, you need to be perfect," I rest in Christ's comforting expectation, "You have done what you could." When I make a mistake and feel ashamed, I don't dwell on it now. I take it to Christ, lay it at his feet in prayer, and walk away from it.

I still want to do well but the pressure is more manageable now, and even helpful. I'm not afraid of failing any longer, as long as I've done my best. I cut myself only that one time, and now see how wrong and pointless that was. The relief I got was so brief, and it was followed by even greater shame. When I'm tempted to do this again, I now think of Christ's wounds for me that cover my failures. That helps me make better choices.

## TURNING THE KEY

If unrealistic expectations or perfectionism are causing you anxiety and depression, you need to ask a number of questions:

1. Where is this expectation coming from? Is it from myself, from my parents or siblings, from my teachers, from my friends, from social media, or from the culture?
2. When you are overwhelmed with "shoulds," ask yourself where each "should" is coming from. Is it unrealistic? Is it impossible? Is it just imagined? Is it from me, a self-imposed "should"? Would God ask me to do this? In this way you can reduce your "shoulds" to manageable numbers.
3. Why is this expectation impacting me so much? What's driving it? Is it pride, desire for control, wanting to please others, trying to impress others, ambition, fear of failure, overestimating my abilities, or something else?

**Write out Matthew 11:29 and memorize it.**

_____

_____

_____

_____

**Prayer**

*Lord Jesus, sometimes I put a heavy yoke on myself or I let others' expectations crush me. Help me to put your yoke on and learn from you. I thank you that, compared to everyone else, your yoke, your expectations, are easy and your burden is light. Enable me to accept my limitations, and when I've done what I can, help me to rest in your "she has done what she could." Amen.*

# 17

# PARALYZED PAM

I hate making decisions. It's so scary. I mean, what if I get it wrong? It will be an utter disaster. If I pick the wrong boyfriend, I could end up in a terrible marriage and be unhappy for the rest of my life. If I choose the wrong college, I might not get my dream job.

But I don't have problems with just big decisions; I can't handle small ones either. What will I wear? What friend will I hang out with? How should I respond to this text? And on and on and on.

It paralyzes me. I end up deciding nothing and doing nothing. It even makes me ill. I get stomach pain and migraines. I can't eat and I can't sleep. And if I ever do make a decision, I can't stop thinking about it. What if I made the wrong choice, and it ruins my life?

I'm doubting myself all the time, and lately I've been doubting and questioning God. Sometimes I wonder if he exists, but I'm afraid to say this to anyone.

—*Pam*

## The Key of Problem-Solving

Pam is right. During the teen years we have to start making a lot of decisions for ourselves, which can be a scary process. However, there is a way to take some of the worry, fear, and confusion out of our problem-solving and decision-making.

Here's the seven-step process that Pam's counselor taught her over a number of weeks.

### STEP 1: CONFIDENCE

We start with building confidence in God. God has planned our lives and wants us to know and follow his plan. He has, therefore, given his children many comforting and encouraging promises. For example, this promise in the book of James has helped many Christians: "If any of you lacks wisdom, let him ask of God, who gives to all liberally and without reproach, and it will be given to him" (James 1:5 NKJV). That should give us great confidence as we make decisions.

### STEP 2: COMMUNE

The foundation of a life guided by God is a life that is lived close to God. Look at how King Solomon connected God's guidance with trusting in God and acknowledging him in all our ways: "Trust in the LORD with all your heart, / And lean not on your own understanding; / In all your ways acknowledge Him, / And He shall direct your paths" (Proverbs 3:5–6 NKJV).

We cannot expect God to give us guidance for life if we are not living our lives for him and with him. The basics of daily Bible reading and prayer and weekly worship services at our local church are the bedrock of drawing us near to God and keeping us close to him. When we aim at his glory more than money, success, and happiness, he will guide us to the target.

### STEP 3: COMMANDMENTS

Sometimes when we say, "Lord, why won't you show me your will for me?" he replies, "Why won't you do my will when you do know it?" Sometimes we try to find out God's will for our future while we are disobeying his will in the present.

Paul says, "Therefore do not be unwise, but understand what the will of the Lord is" (Eph. 5:17 NKJV). Notice that the verses before and after this verse are about obedience to God. We cannot expect God to guide us in areas we are unsure of if we are not following him in areas that are clear to us.

## STEP 4: COMPARE

Having laid this spiritual foundation of faith, fellowship, and faithfulness, we then begin to look at the various options in front of us. Write out each possible choice or action, and underneath write the pros and cons, the costs and benefits, the advantages and disadvantages of each. That gets the jumble of thoughts and desires into a more logical and organized form, which makes decisions and solutions much easier.

It's helpful to remember that some decisions are small even though they feel big. Choosing a summer job, for instance, may feel big in the moment, but ultimately, it is a three-month commitment and may not be life-altering.

## STEP 5: CUT

Once we've got the options on paper, we can begin to eliminate the least likely possibilities. We may not yet know what the right choice is, but some of the wrong options are more obvious. That reduces the number of options, giving greater clarity. Sometimes the right answer pops out as we do this. There may be a couple that are equally good choices. That's fine. Either path will work out well.

## STEP 6: CONSULT

The wisest man in the world once said, "Where there is no counsel, the people fall; / But in the multitude of counselors there is safety" (Proverbs 11:14 NKJV). How many falls and fails would have been prevented if only we had asked for and taken advice!

Although some friends might be a help here, when it comes to important decisions, it's best to talk to people older and wiser than we are, especially mature Christians such as our pastor, elder, or parents. When you talk with them, explain your thought processes up to this point and the different paths that you could take.

Here's an example of the kinds of questions to talk over when making college and career choices:

- *What talents has God given you?* God is not calling you to do something that he has not equipped you for. You'll never be a carpenter if you can't work with your hands. You'll never be a teacher if you hate kids.
- *What desires, interests, strengths, and passions has he given you?* God will sometimes call us to do something surprising, but he usually works by giving us a passion or a strength and directing that into a vocation.
- *What opportunities has he given you?* Has he already given you openings to exercise your gifts and talents? God may call you to do something completely different from what you are doing, but he usually takes what he has already developed in you and develops it further along the same trajectory.
- *What encouragements has he given you?* Have others recognized your gifts and talents in this area? Have you had any indicators of progress or success in this?

Sometimes just talking about these questions will give clarity. Often these advisors will see things that we never thought about.

### STEP 7: COMMIT

Make the decision. Yes, eventually we have to decide and act. Avoiding a decision just makes things worse and fertilizes our anxiety. Sometimes we have to make a decision even when it's not 100 percent clear what that decision should be. We may not be sure of our ultimate destination, but we have to take a first step, and we do so in faith that God will continue to guide each step. Taking a risk or moving forward gives God an opportunity to bless. And even if a decision turns out to be wrong, God will use it for good (Romans 8:28).

## Update from Pam

These seven steps have been so helpful to me. I must be honest: the first three were missing from my life. When I got my relationship with God right, decision-making and problem-solving became a lot easier. I felt more confident and hopeful.

I still don't like making decisions, but when I feel paralysis setting in, I follow the steps and trust God. Writing out the options with the pros and cons clears my head, and usually the right answer becomes more obvious. I keep these sheets of paper and go back over them at times to encourage me with how God has helped me solve problems and make good decisions in the past.

Although I don't go through all the seven steps with every little decision of life, I've found that the little decisions are easier and quicker as a result of using the seven steps with the big decisions.

My counselor encouraged me to talk to my pastor about my spiritual doubts and questions. He was really nice. He said it was very common in teen years to go through a time of doubt and questioning, but that if I talked honestly about it and prayed over it, God would use it to strengthen my faith.

I'm moving forward in my life now, and I'm confident that God will guide me to the right destination. Even if I take a wrong turn here and there, I know God will work it all out because I am living for him and with him.

## TURNING THE KEY

Pick a challenging issue that you are facing, and work your way through the seven steps to make a decision. This will help reduce fear and build confidence for future bigger decisions.

**Write out Proverbs 3:6 and memorize it.**

_____

_____

_____

_____

**Prayer**

*You, God, are my guide. Please lead me in every area of life. Make your will known to me and help me to do it. I trust you to help me make right decisions and overrule for my good even if I mess up. Amen.*

# 18

# LONELY LUKE

My dad is in the military, so we've moved around a lot. I think I've changed school six times in ten years. I find it hard to make friends, and I get nervous and tense in crowds. I don't mix with anyone at school, and most people just leave me alone, which is fine. It's actually harder at church, especially at the youth group, because they try to involve me in everything, including group discussions. The last time I went bright red and could hardly talk. Everyone laughed. I felt so dumb. I don't ever want to go to church again. It's so awkward and embarrassing. I can worship God at home.

—*Luke*

## The Key of Church

How do we help Luke? We can understand his feelings about church, can't we? Going to church can be hard when we're anxious or depressed. It's especially difficult for people like Luke who have a social anxiety disorder.

But, as I told Luke, while he had valid reasons to avoid church and stay home, there are better reasons for him to go. I also gave him practical tips to make church attendance more manageable and doable. But, first, why go to church when you're suffering with anxiety or depression?

## CHURCH BRINGS GOD NEAR

In previous chapters, we've seen how much peace comes through Scripture, Christ, and prayer. We can enjoy much of that in our own private and family devotions.

However, God has chosen church as the place where he especially makes himself known. He is there among his gathered people in a special way. Scripture is read and explained, Christ and his salvation are preached and praised, prayer is offered and answered. God draws especially near in these public services of worship.

It would be a pity not to use this means of healing. It would be like having a huge pharmacy of medicine down the road but choosing not to use it when your doctor has given you a prescription. The thing we dread is actually where we can find healing and help.

## CHURCH REMINDS US OF OTHERS

Anxiety and depression isolate us and turn us in on ourselves. We can get so self-focused that we forget the needs of others. We think we are the only one in the world with problems.

When we come to church, we see lots of people with lots of problems, and realize that we are not unique or alone in our suffering. We begin to be thankful for the mercies we do have rather than focus on what we don't have. We even begin to pray for and with others who are facing their own challenges.

There's something incredibly therapeutic about getting the focus off ourselves and on to others. Our whole worldview changes when we put God at the center and include the needs of others in our view of the world.

## CHURCH HELPS US TO PRAISE GOD

While we can try to praise God on our own at home, it's usually much easier when we join with other worshipers. The sound and sight of others singing praises to God carries us along, loosens our tongues, and expands our lungs.

There's something so calming and pacifying about songs that remind us of who God is, and what he has done, is doing, and will yet do. Even if we cannot yet add our voices to the choir of praise, we can let the waves of song wash over us and carry us forward and upward.

## CHURCH IS A CARING COMMUNITY

In chapter 13, we noted the important role of healthy friendships in nurturing peace in our lives. Church is often the best place for finding and building these friendships. There we can find people our own age who share our values and beliefs and who often face similar struggles. It's a great blessing to get together with them each Sunday, share our stories, pray together, and help and hug one another.

But we'll also find older people there who have been through many more struggles and difficulties in life and are willing to help us—maybe the youth leader, pastor, or a counselor. Or it may be just someone you sit beside. Pray that the Lord would bring the right person into your life. You don't need lots of friends at church, but to have a couple of sympathetic friends in the faith is invaluable.

## BABY STEPS

Given that church is the best of places and the worst of places at times, how can we maximize the advantages and minimize the disadvantages? How can we make it easier to go to church and benefit from it? Here's the practical advice I gave to Luke. I encouraged him to view going to church as a "fear project," a challenge to overcome and an opportunity for growth.

- *Start.* Begin with one service on a Sunday. Your church may have two services, youth groups, Sunday school, and other activities. Don't try to do it all. Start small with one service, and rebuild your confidence.
- *Go in a few minutes late, sit in the back, and leave a few minutes early.* You will get the benefit of the worship service without the stress of having to interact with people

and engaging in small talk. If you get panicky, you can leave without others seeing.

- *Protect.* Ask one of your parents or a friend to sit with you so that you don't feel alone. They can also protect you if people start surrounding you or asking you lots of questions about where you've been.

- *Personalize.* Try to make the words of the praises and prayers your own. These are ready-made songs and prayers that you can own and send to God when you cannot find the mental strength to do it yourself. Try to hear God's word read and preached as God's voice to you.

- *Build.* After a few weeks of getting used to this, you can begin to build. Stay after church for five minutes and talk briefly to a few friends. Maybe add the youth group eventually, and so on. Slowly and gradually increase your exposure to what you makes you anxious.

- *Trust.* If you start feeling panicky in church, drink some water, take some deep breaths, pray to God for calm, and trust him to keep you.

- *Gratitude.* Thank God for each time he helps you to take a step forward, and use that to encourage you that he will continue to help and strengthen you going forward.

- *Serve.* As you get stronger, begin to think about how you can serve others. Is there someone else you can help? Maybe there's a child with special needs that you can look after. Maybe there's a harassed mother whose kids you could watch for ten minutes while she chats with friends. If we can forget ourselves and think about serving others instead, much of our social anxiety will reduce.

---

### Update from Luke

I've actually quite enjoyed my "fear project." Breaking it up into small steps helped a lot, and each time I managed to go forward a little, it encouraged me to go further. My counselor gave me three questions to ask myself before going into social settings:

- "What's the worst that could happen?"
- "What's the likelihood of this happening?"
- "What will you do if it does happen?"

I've started writing down the answers to these questions, which helps me face these situations more rationally and calmly. It helps me to see that many of my fears are unfounded, and that even if the worst does happen, I have a simple plan to act upon.

I've also started putting the chairs away after church. It takes me and some other guys about fifteen minutes, but I'm getting to know them now and it does feel good to actually be helpful again. I'm trying to forget myself more and think about others instead. Going to church is getting easier.

## TURNING THE KEY

1. Each Sunday you go to church write down:
   - A line from a song that helped you.
   - A truth from the sermon that spoke to you.
   - Something kind that someone said or did for you.
   - Something kind you said or did for someone else.
2. Start a fear project.
   - Identify what you are afraid of (e.g., social gatherings).
   - Make a plan to slowly and gradually confront and overcome the fear.
   - Expose yourself gradually to more and more challenging situations (e.g., start with a one-to-one conversation).
   - Record your progress at each step to encourage you.
   - As you conquer each fear, you will have a testimony to God's faithfulness.
3. Start a service project.
   Although it's the last thing you might feel like doing, research has shown that volunteering helps a lot with depression and anxiety. Ask your pastor or youth group leader if there's a way you can serve at church.

Visualize a Fear Ladder, where you are gradually moving up toward your fear. Ideally it should have somewhere between eight to ten steps. You should always do something like this under the supervision of a trained counselor or mental health professional.

**Write out 1 Peter 5:7 and memorize it.**

_____

_____

_____

_____

**Prayer**

*Faithful God, I confess that I don't want to go to church. It makes me scared to even think about it. I know this needs to change and that you will help me. Hold me as I take these baby steps in my fear project. I thank you that you care for me, and therefore I cast all my cares upon you. Amen.*

# Conclusion
# GROWING FREEDOM

You started this book in the bondage of anxiety and depression. Maybe you despaired of ever experiencing peace and joy again. Having read the book and discovered so many liberating keys, you have new hope of freedom. But what do you do now? What's the next step?

## First Steps Taken

First, by understanding anxiety and depression better, you've already taken the most important steps to freedom. Before reading this book, you probably had no idea about what was happening to you. You were confused and perplexed. It was like being blindfolded on a bungee cord, not knowing what was happening or what was coming next. But now you understand it much more. Although you may still be on the bungee, the blindfold has been removed, you can see more clearly what's happening to you, and the ups and downs are getting less. That itself is a big step forward.

Also, you now see that there are many keys of freedom. Prior to this book, you may have felt hopeless and helpless. "I don't know why I feel like this, and there's nothing I can do about it." But now you see that God has provided many solutions. There are many simple actions you can take. There are things you can do to make things better. That's so empowering and encouraging, isn't it? Understanding your bondage and discovering keys to unlock your life are big steps.

## One at a Time

The worst thing you could do is try to use all the keys at once. Instead, pick one or two to try at a time. Ask yourself which ones appealed to you most. Which made most sense to you? Start with those keys, and try one at a time for a week or so until you get used to it and you feel some healing. Then you can pick up another and add it to your key ring.

If you are finding one too difficult to use at this point or it's not that effective, just leave it for the moment and try another. What works great for some people may not do anything for someone else. One thing I can tell you is that the vast majority of teens with anxiety and depression get better if they use the keys God has provided. But you have to use the keys regularly, maybe even for the rest of your life.

## Commit to Study

Getting free of these emotional chains will not only change your whole future, it will probably boost your GPA as well! That's why you should view this as the most important subject to study at the moment.

One of the best ways to keep at this is to schedule a time each day when you will reread the book and work on the exercises. View it like studying for math or biology. Put a fifteen- to twenty-minute block in your study schedule each day, ideally the same time each day, and soon it will be a normal part of your routine.

## Perfect Weakness

As I said earlier, almost all the teens who use the keys God has provided experience significant relief and even complete freedom from anxiety and depression. It takes longer for some than others, and some people are vulnerable in this area for the rest of their lives. Yes, you can enjoy freedom for many months or even years, but then for one reason or another, you may find yourself back in the darkness again. That can be frustrating, but it's one of the ways that God humbles us, keeps us dependent on him, and shows us his strength and grace. So make this your last memory verse:

And He said to me, "My grace is sufficient for you, for My strength is made perfect in weakness." Therefore most gladly I will rather boast in my infirmities, that the power of Christ may rest upon me. (2 Corinthians 12:9 NKJV)

We sometimes think we would be better witnesses if we were able to be happy and strong all the time. But often God chooses to show his power in our weakness so that people see his strength not ours, his grace not our success.

And if you do relapse, be assured that the depression and anxiety probably won't last so long or go so deep. That's because you now know you can get out of it and what to do. Just go back to the keys and start using them again. In fact, if you do have a tendency toward depression and anxiety, you will probably want to make this book a lifelong companion and keep using the keys even in the good times, in order to prevent reoccurrence.

This book has covered the basics of depression and anxiety, but if you want to read more or learn more, please visit whyamIfeeling likethis.com, where you'll find many videos and articles that will help you further on this journey to freedom.

# SCRIPTURE INDEX

# Also Available from David Murray

Many parents of teenagers know the feeling: instead of the confident, happy, hopeful young adult they hoped to raise, they see an anxious, depressed, scared teen. Counselor David Murray offers spiritual encouragement and practical direction for parents and other adults to guide teenagers through anxiety and depression.

For more information, visit **crossway.org**.

# Notes

**Notes**

**Notes**

# Notes

# Notes

**Notes**

**Notes**

# Notes

**Notes**